SELLING

IN TODAY'S ECONOMY

SELLING

IN TODAY'S ECONOMY

*Applying Laws of Physics
and Performance Art
to Gain the Cutting Edge*

J. M. Barry and Lawrence Coats

iUniverse, Inc.
Bloomington

Selling in Today's Economy
Applying Laws of Physics and Performance
Art to Gain the Cutting Edge

iUniverse books may be ordered through booksellers or by contacting:

iUniverse
1663 Liberty Drive
Bloomington, IN 47403
www.iuniverse.com
1-800-Authors (1-800-288-4677)

Because of the dynamic nature of the Internet, any web addresses or links contained in this book may have changed since publication and may no longer be valid. The views expressed in this work are solely those of the author and do not necessarily reflect the views of the publisher, and the publisher hereby disclaims any responsibility for them.

Any people depicted in stock imagery provided by Thinkstock are models, and such images are being used for illustrative purposes only.

Certain stock imagery © Thinkstock.

ISBN: 978-1-4620-5555-5 (sc)
ISBN: 978-1-4620-5553-1 (e)

Library of Congress Control Number: 2011917150

Printed in the United States of America

iUniverse rev. date: 1/09/2012

To Eric Moulton for his encouragement and for providing us with a "coefficient of friction," to Zig Zigler and Tony Robbins for their inspiration to us over the past few decades, to Jeff Meier for his support and encouragement, to Emma Fontes for being there, and to our children who have taught us as much about selling as anyone else

Contents

Contents

The world economy is hurting more than ever before! Many salespeople are or may soon be without work! Companies can pick and choose from the best of the best sales talent all competing for the same jobs. In today's challenged economy it's time to raise the sales bar!

INTRODUCTION

Fasten Your Seatbelt; You're
Going for a Ride

This book is for those who want to be the best at selling. Who sells? *Everybody sells!* If you want someone to do what you want them to do, *you are selling!*

Even pets sell. Pets sell to their owners! Felines are some of the best sellers ever seen in action. Dogs aren't half bad either, although not nearly as good as cats. In fact, they both sell without uttering a single intelligible word, something all sales professionals should learn to do!

Parents sell to their children. Children sell to adults. Adults sell to their friends. The simple truth is that in any given situation there is a whole lot of selling going on!

The information in this book will enable you to get your point across (selling) more effectively in today's tough marketplace and get others to do what you want them to do (buying) far more frequently.

Whether you are a hairstylist, a CEO, a pharmacist, a construction worker, a lover, an artist, a mom or a dad, or even (God forbid) a sales professional, *read this book!*

The world economy is hurting more than ever before! Gone are the days when dressing professionally, body language, asking the right questions, following the classic sales fundamentals, using the correct closing technique, listening to motivational tapes, following *The Seven Habits of Highly Effective People*, disciplined cold calling, and so on will get you the sale. All of these aspects are just as important as they were before, but in today's challenged economy it's time to raise the sales bar! It's time to reengineer and sharpen your sales skills to a fine-honed cutting edge.

The world today is a tough place for sales talent. Many salespeople are or may soon be without work! Companies can pick and choose from the best of the best sales talent all competing for the same jobs and then pay them lower commissions on top of it.

Customers have a tighter grip on their wallets than ever before. Times are uncertain. Smart customers no longer believe that a purchase is urgent. They know business is slow. They believe it is a buyer's market, and they are correct! As sales athletes, we have to be that much better to make sales and, subsequently, a lucrative income.

The authors have been in the sales business for fifty combined years. They built themselves up decades ago from "rookies" to top sales athletes to trainers for major companies.

The unique, creative, and unusual elements of sales technique supplied in this book have been used, tested, and proven by the sales divisions of Marriott, Ritz-Carlton, Starwood, Four Seasons, Playground, EMI Music Publishing, and a variety of lesser-known companies.

What makes this book distinctly different from any other is the diverse background of its two authors. You will be given insight into the "secrets" of their unique combined wisdom, which has been coveted by large corporations for over a decade—the same "secrets" that have been utilized by the most successful professionals in theater, film, and sales arenas for many decades.

J. M. Barry was classically trained in theater and studied for fifteen years with the best acting coaches currently in the industry: William H. Macy (Academy Award–nominated actor); David Mamet (Pulitzer Prize–winning author of numerous plays, including *Glengarry Glen Ross* and *American Buffalo*, and veteran stage and film director); Steven Schachter, film director and screenwriter; and Harold Guskin, world-renowned private acting coach to iconic stage, television, and film stars.

So why on earth would that kind of insight be beneficial regarding selling? What does acting training have to do with selling?

Everything!

Have you ever received an award or recognition for your great sales performance? Have you ever received performance management when you weren't selling so well? Why do sales organizations use the word "performance"?

Because that is exactly what selling is. It is performing. It is acting. Acting is *not* pretending. Acting is taking an action. In fact, great selling is really performance art! Your stage is anywhere you happen to be selling. Your audience is your customer. As sales athletes, we all know that we need to keep our "pitch" fresh. Though we may repeat our pitch (script) time and time again, year after year, it needs to be as fresh, exciting, and instilled with passion and belief as the first time we were in front of our "audience," the customer. Stale or canned sales presentations translate into "no sales."

Can you imagine what the performances would be like for long-running theater productions such as *Cats*, *Les Misérables*, or *Wicked* if those talented performers did not receive proper training on how to keep their performance electric and sizzling every time they walked out in front of their audience, even at their one thousandth performance?

Unlike any other sales book, *Selling in Today's Economy* will reveal to you the "secrets" that the most successful actors use to keep their performances "fresh" and powerful. It will provide you with the tools to keep your sales performance fresh, passionate, infectious, contagious, and as full of belief and raw passion as the first day you went out onto the sales line as a rank "green pea" and perhaps made that sale via your pure, unadulterated, profound excitement.

Lawrence Coats has studied with and worked alongside the best sales trainers and entrepreneurs in the country. He has consulted on some of the most successful real estate developments in the United States including Hawaii, Canada, and the Caribbean. His sales performance on its own is beyond compare, unbeaten and legendary in many companies. He has repeatedly led sales teams and divisions to great financial successes. Through his years of hard work in the sales industry, Coats has witnessed the critical changes we have all seen in the styles of communications. Most significant is the shift in the last ten years from faxes and landlines to BlackBerries, e-mails, and the small bytes of texting and tweeting, all of which have limited and fractured the actual contact time sales professionals are able to procure from their extremely time-crunched and discerning customers.

To make matters worse these days, by the time you meet your customers, they know as much about your product and the competition as you do. The Internet has brought information to their fingertips at the speed of light. They all use it diligently, just as you do! Customers are better informed now. They need to be acknowledged for that and treated as such.

In the time-crunched world of today, where we all rely so heavily on e-mail, texts, Facebook, tweets, and quick calls on our mobile phones between other engagements, we are lucky to get more than a couple of minutes at a time with a customer with whom we are trying to build a meaningful and trusting relationship. The fact is that we may never meet them face-to-face before closing the deal.

Mr. Coats has created proven systems enabling the application of great sales techniques to today's communication technologies.

Great selling is performance art! Your stage is anywhere you happen to be selling. Selling in Today's Economy will reveal to you the "secrets" that the most successful actors use to keep their performances fresh, powerful, competitive, and cutting edge.

Selling Inside-Out

For many, up until now, selling has been an outside-in learning process. You learn the skills. You buy the clothes. If you do certain things, you will be successful. Not anymore! The world has shifted.

That shift is being rammed down your throat by speed-of-light Internet and e-commerce. Opportunity abounds! However, we are all expendable if we don't change with the times and turn selling inside-out.

What is selling inside-out? It is creating a context within you through which everything else is focused. It is creating the correct emotional state (attitude) first and foremost and then having absolute control and laser-like focus with it. When you have that thirty-second opportunity to make contact with your very busy customer, your contact must be strategic and powerful enough to lead you to the next step.

Selling today is being vulnerable and emotionally available. The more vulnerable you are when you get that forty-five-second contact byte, the more powerful your emotional impact will be on your customer. It is using all those learned sales techniques and transforming them through the heART of your inner psyche. It is the actor's way—the way to take an action honestly and powerfully and, in that moment, making it count profoundly.

Then it is using all that action appropriately within the context of the segmented sales presentation as it exists today. In the current marketplace, that is the only way for a salesperson to become indispensible. You are human. You must become *more* human. You must revel in your humanity while at the same time being the strategic hunter/warrior. You must take *all* your technique and run it through your heART center. You must become powerful in your ability to project through your heART as well as vulnerable and emotionally available. It sounds all "psycho-touchy-feely," doesn't it? Well, guess what—it is!

And if you work hard at it and practice, as any sales athlete should always be doing, you will be able to infuse your customers with a previously unobtainable intensity of irrefutable passion, belief, and true vulnerability. It's just like that rank beginner who made his first sale right out of the gate with almost zero skill or knowledge, with just raw enthusiasm and passion. If you can "unlearn" what you think you know and reengineer your sales process, your customers will respond to you in kind. Like a fallen tree in a raging river, they will be compelled to move along with you.

If you want to be successful in sales in this economy,
then you need to read this book!

CHAPTER I

Eclectic Electric Conversations

- ➢ Customers have changed the way they communicate.
- ➢ In today's market, one must be proficient in all methods of communication.
- ➢ Begin to understand how too much information can become detrimental.

By the time you interact with your customers, they may have as many facts about your product and the competition as you do. The Internet has brought information to their fingertips at the speed of light, and they all use it! Customers are smarter, and they need to be acknowledged for that and treated as such.

With text, tweet, e-mail, and mobile phone, the sales process with most customers is segmented at best. We get two minutes with a customer as she runs between business meetings, a text the following day requesting more info on a given aspect of the product, a ninety-second phone opportunity two days later as she drops the kids at soccer practice while on the way to her martial arts class, and a Facebook contact because she wanted you to become her "friend"—and maybe, if you are really lucky, you might actually get to meet her one day (probably not) before she drops three million on your private jet sale.

Consider this analogy: Rarely these days—most of the time in the old days—are sales presentations akin to a live theater presentation. The curtain goes up. There is Act I, Act II, and the finale, Act III. Curtain goes down; applause! Sales presentations used to be much like theater. They were linear from point A to point Z during which you could perform a structured script/presentation. That was then. This is now.

These days most sales presentations can be compared to film production. There is an extended shooting schedule that has to make sense economically and logistically for the cast and crew involved. Each day there is a different scene to shoot. The scenes are not usually in the chronological order of the script. They are nonlinear, depending upon the needs of the production (customer and product). Day one you are shooting (discussing) a scene three pages from the end of the story, and day two you are shooting page four near the beginning of the script. With our customers' crazy schedules and fingertip knowledge off the Internet, just like a film production, their needs can have us all over the place if we are not strategic in our interactions.

> *Regardless of which page of script is being shot on any given day, everyone in the cast and crew needs to know where he is in the overall concept regarding the linear order of the script (presentation) and character development (six sales fundamentals), regardless of what order of shooting occurs as the film production (sale) progresses.*

Eclectic Electric Modus Operandi

How do you know how to communicate with a customer? Do you use e-mails, texts, mail, face-to-face conversations, or phone calls as a preferred mode of communication? Many times a sales professional will ignore the key signals of how to communicate with a customer and never get a response from him. It's not that the customer is not interested; it simply is that we are communicating with the customer in a manner that is not his preference. With the evolution of the Internet, one can see many examples of how the market has changed drastically in the past five years.

Just look at Internet dating. These sites barely existed ten years ago. Now there are numerous sites that one can join to browse for "dates." Some of these sites are geared toward finding your soul mate, while others are truly just dating sites. These sites in the past ten years have exploded with memberships, because people don't have the time to meet people in public. Or due to logistic circumstance, they don't have the ability to meet people. They join these sites, review profiles, flirt a little, and try to engage in conversations. It has become a huge success and is very popular due to the efficiency of the dating process. One might even say it's a great elimination process for those you don't want to date. Ultimately, through a little research, discovery, and electronic conversation, couples move to actually meeting face-to-face for a "date." Are there any direct correlations to how the sales industry has changed in the past ten years? Do you think it will continue to change going forward?

The current sales professional must incorporate some of those habits that we see in the Internet dating sites and apply them into their presentation. A large percentage of our leads today come through the Internet and phone, with the largest majority of those being from the Internet.

So what's the right mode of communication? If a potential customer contacted your company to inquire about your product, then use the same mode of communication for the response and the initial conversations. Therefore, if they contacted you via e-mail, respond via e-mail. Then stay with electronic conversation for as long as the customer wishes. When beginning this way, a good clue that you are making proper advances is when the customer asks you to call them on the phone!

The following chart outlines when it is possible to communicate with a customer using various aspects of sales fundamentals. Some may be better than others, but the fact remains that done properly there are many ways to communicate with our customers through technology without throwing away the primary constructs of proper sales technique.

Communication Mode Comparison

	Email	Phone	Face to Face	Mail
Meet and Greet	•	•	•	•
Warm-Up	•	•	•	•
Intent Statement	•	•	•	•
Use of Next Step Approach	•	•	•	•
Inflection of response	•	•	•	•
Creating Urgency	•	•	•	•
Thorough Discovery	•	•	•	•
Advocating the Product	•	•	•	•
Closing the Transaction	•	•	•	•
Paperwork	•	•	•	•
Referral Program	•	•	•	•
Pacing the Presentation	•	•	•	•
Communicate with Both Spouses	•	•	•	•
Body Language			•	
Vocal Tonality		•	•	
Create & Articulate a Strategic Response	•			•
Combine with Other Modes of Communication	•	•	•	•

E-mail, without a doubt, will allow the sales professional to establish the pace of the presentation and provide ample time to craft the perfect statement or question that elicits the response you want from your customer. E-mail also tells you a lot about the customer. Restructuring and rewording your presentation to incorporate all forms of communication is achievable and highly recommended. However, start with your e-mail! It will create improved dialogue that generally translates to a better phone and face-to-face presentation. Less is more, and strategy rules!

E-mail is a powerful source for communication. Simply put, it is an electronic conversation surgically crafted. And yes, an entire presentation can take place with a sale as an outcome strictly through electronic communication. However, in most cases, a combination of styles and methods of communication ultimately establish the presentation. Therefore, it is necessary to pay close attention to your e-mail. It is an extension of your voice, so choose your words carefully.

Can you think of some leads that were given to you that you responded to with a random e-mail without thinking strategically and economically? Did you keep the first series of e-mails short—four sentences at most—and always end the e-mail with a question? Did you ever send an e-mail that did not get a response and when you called you never got them to pick up the phone, so you discounted their interest? Do you think it could have been your initial e-mail that destroyed any chance of future communication?

Electronic conversation can be easily related to a face-to-face conversation. The analogy would be as if you just met someone for the first time and you started a conversation. In the beginning of a brand-new relationship, the conversation, if it develops, is usually a back-and-forth conversation of short statements by the parties involved. It rarely is successful if one party takes off on a five- or ten-minute download about themselves or a specific topic. That's not a constructive conversation. It's a lecture! It is boring, with too much to absorb that is not relevant to the other person.

If the conversation starts as a back-and-forth interaction of short sentences, it typically involves easily answered questions, especially in the beginning. As the relationship evolves, the give-and-take sessions can become a little longer and more in-depth. The questions can become more personal and require more of a thought process. The questions flow naturally. The answers are then meaningful. The opposite would be a deposition of feature benefits or an interrogation of discovery. A great conversation, if successful, leads to another meeting or conversation at a later time. This is true with electronic conversation as well.

Look at some of your old e-mail chains. Do you see any places where you could have improved the conversation? Can you clearly explain the strategic reason why you chose every word in your e-mail? Can you clearly see where you were going? What was your strategy? Was your e-mail too long (a dissertation)? Did it have too many questions (an interrogation)? Did you take the time to make it more concise and far more strategic? Or did you just respond without careful consideration by loving the sound of your own rambling thoughts?

Sell the Shave—Not the Razor

The delivery and explanation of a highly complex product requires the skill of a sales athlete to simplify the clarification to the customer. From the beginning it needs to be "simple and easy" to understand. This is accomplished by layering your presentation correctly, layering your discovery questions so that they are relevant and interesting, advocating the product carefully by providing a base of what the product is and how the product will work seamlessly for him, and then advocating some ideas so that he can leverage his ownership of what you are selling. In the end, the customer wants to know if it will work for him, *not how it works.*

> *The delivery and explanation of a highly complex product requires the skill of a sales athlete to simplify the clarification to the customer. The customer wants to know if it will work for him, not how it works.*

Star Wars Defense Systems

I met an individual who worked under President Reagan in the 1980s. This individual had the task of determining how to use laser refraction in outer space to send laser beams from a satellite in space back to earth to intercept nuclear warheads that could be deployed from Russia. This project was called Star Wars. This individual was a nuclear and space refraction physicist. He had a team of scientists who addressed this opportunity for nearly four years. Star Wars never developed due to the fact that laser beams get bent in space and as such don't have the accuracy to precisely intercept a nuclear warhead that is traveling at 50,000 feet above sea level at 800 mph. Basically, it can't work.

When I was talking to this individual, he was sensitive to my limited knowledge of special laser beam refraction, so he simply explained it in layman's terms. It took about five minutes. He mentioned that he'd just had a five-day conference in Washington, DC, that included eight hours each day explaining why it didn't work and what the Star Wars project limitations were. After those meetings had concluded, he was required to give President Reagan a briefing on the conclusions of their exhaustive study. Do you think President Reagan needed forty hours of technical babble? It took this scientist friend of mine ten minutes to explain it succinctly enough so that President Reagan understood all the implications of the faulty technology.

Given the chance, the professional salesperson often dumps so much useless data into a customer's head that they can't and won't make a decision. The worst thing a professional salesperson can do is confuse the customer with mindless babble ... *especially when the product can work for him.* It is just a poor presentation, and you have probably deterred that customer from doing what you want him to do. There is also a ripple effect from this confusing way of presenting your ideas. The customer has friends who could very likely be great referrals, and now that channel of business has been eliminated.

KEY POINTS

- ➤ Like it or not, the world communicates electronically.
- ➤ Involve yourself in new communication formats.
- ➤ Be surgical in all electronic conversation and avoid data dumping.

CHAPTER 2

Customer Knowledge + Sales Wisdom = $$$$$

> ➢ You may have years of knowledge of a product or service, but you need wisdom for optimal results.
> ➢ You only know what you really and truly know!
> ➢ Be comfortable in your own skin.

In most disciplines, sales included, there are four levels of expertise.

> ➢ The Unconscious Incompetent
> ➢ The Conscious Incompetent
> ➢ The Unconscious Competent
> ➢ The Conscious Competent

The *Unconscious Incompetent* individual is quite simply clueless about what his or her task is and how to go about it. We have all run into these individuals. They are the useless nephews of union bosses hired onto the company payroll in positions for which they have no skill or training, customer service persons who wouldn't be able to assist you if their lives depended upon it, politicians who are so ill-suited to their elected posts that they stand no chance for reelection, or tone-deaf television actors who think they will make a go of it as a recording artist. Worst of all, they think they are perfectly suited for their tasks and have no idea how they are truly misplaced.

The *Conscious Incompetent* person is a *giant* step up. He is clueless and readily admits it. Conscious Incompetence is actually a great state of being. This is an individual who is ripe for learning. His "cup is empty." He could, if hungry enough to work hard and grow through experience, become the next big success story.

The *Unconscious Competent* is sadly not a good place to be at all. This person has been cursed with success in their chosen or delegated field—sometimes via dumb luck; sometimes because they made a series of choices that brought positive results. However, put enough monkeys in a room with enough typewriters for a long enough time and one of them will eventually write a beautiful sonnet. As a result of his success, the unconscious competent's "cup is full." They are incapable of listening to criticism or learning anything. The unconscious competent is eventually doomed to fail and will likely never recover with a career comeback unless he can first embrace the simple fact that he is incompetent due to the very fact that he has absolutely no clue why he was successful.

Conscious Competents are complex and rare individuals. They are duplicitous in their consciousness. While they are masters at their crafts and could teach their skills, they are also students of what they do and often feel they know next to nothing. They constantly thirst for personal growth and improvement in their skills. Their cups are both full and empty at the same time. They're rarely satisfied with their achievements. These individuals are easy to spot. They are prolific producers filled with tireless passion and hunger to learn more and constantly raise the bar on their results. They have a vast knowledge of their work and, more importantly, vast wisdom.

Knowledge Good/Wisdom Great

Wisdom requires that we understand the world in ways that lead to appropriate decisions about what is most important in life. Wisdom is expressed in Native American culture in that the death of their elders is the greatest tragedy for the village. The death of the young is a personal tragedy for the family and those who care deeply, but not for the village. Why? Because when the elderly die, much wisdom is lost, and the fabric of the village sustains a large experiential deficit. When the youngest of the tribe die, the damage to the village's store of wisdom is of minimal impact.

Those with little wisdom can achieve knowledge. They know their subject nonexperientially through study, whether it is on the fossils of the Columbian shale or the works of Shakespeare. But only a fool would ask their advice on any other subject. They lack real experience.

Information is the prime feature of our age. Undigested, ill-understood, and often incorrect statements are culled from sundry sources on the Internet without any idea of how to sift the good from the bad and the indifferent.

Would most students you know really be able to tell you whether what they are being taught is reliable or not? They would struggle. They may say that what they know they studied for years in books. And when told that they believe on the basis of authority only and not through personal experience, they are horrified by that accusation.

Have knowledge, yes, but most importantly have wisdom throughout your entire sales presentation. *You are now the sage for your knowledge-burdened customer!* The knowledge of your product line is undoubtedly extensive; the amount of knowledge is massive. The wisdom is to discover what parts of the product are key to your customers and to take advantage of those features and benefits so they become your buyers—or not. Don't recommend that they purchase your product if it simply wouldn't work for them. They do not possess the wisdom to discern that fact.

> *"Knowledge without wisdom is a pile of books strapped onto the back of a fool." This Japanese proverb indicates that it is important to have knowledge, yes, but most important is to have wisdom throughout your entire sales presentation. You are now the sage for your knowledge-burdened customer!*

Selling Is a No-Pretend Zone

Selling is a "no-pretend zone." Only "know" what you actually really and truly know to be true. Otherwise, empty your cup and be a student of knowledge. When I escaped New York City to the peaceful rural confines of upstate New York, my neighbors quickly made themselves "available" to me. Their feigned kindness was all in an effort to size me up. After all, I was the new "city kid" in their rural neighborhood. One of those visits shall remain forever imprinted in my memory as an example of a trap so many salespeople fall into.

Shortly after we moved in, Tommy Benson knocked on our door one sunny morning and offered to show us around our new 120-acre property. Since he'd lived across the street from our farm his entire life, playing there as a child, he felt that he could give us the lowdown on our new property.

As we walked along, Tommy pointed out this and that with a too-cute childhood story attached to each item. He had never gotten into farming. Instead he opted to take over his father's oil delivery business. Most of the farms in that area were still heated with oil furnaces during their long cold winters. Tommy was really a businessman in quaint rural clothing. He had hands as soft and unspoiled as those of any lady at an opera.

We walked along a large hedgerow of forsythia bordering one of my fields. Forsythia is a lovely spindly green decorative border plant that grows to about eight feet tall each year, produces beautifully delicate yellow flowers in the early spring, and then must be cut down to the ground in the fall for the following year's growth. Tommy looked at that forsythia and boldly stated, "Jimmy, them's sirthythia, and I know everything there is to know about sirthythia." In all the years I lived across the road from Tommy, I never once saw him tending his garden or taking care of his sizeable estate. He always hired people to do that for him, yet he claimed to know everything there is to know.

It was a full two years before I learned from a botanist friend (much to my extreme embarrassment) that they were not called sirthythia. I also realized the only advice I should ever take from my neighbor Tommy Benson was anything having to do with oil heat. From that moment forward, every time I saw Tommy, my opinion of him was slightly diminished.

Orson Welles narrated one of his last films, *F for Fake*. It was an exposé on the concept of "experts." The film's theme was essentially about being diligently cautious of anyone who claims to be an expert, because most often that claim is a clear indication that the opposite is probably more true.

That goes for any one of us trying to get a point across to our customers, kids, family, or friends. *We only know what we actually really and truly know.* If we're merely repeating something we've heard or are pretending to know something we are only vaguely familiar with or worst of all are fabricating data because we are afraid to say, "I don't know," then we are definitely setting ourselves up for looking foolish and losing credibility!

Taking that one step further, this also pertains to who you present yourself to be when taking action to get someone to do what you want them to do (selling).

Be yourself. Unless you are a highly trained actor with a closet full of acting awards, do not attempt to be anything other than genuinely *you*. Obviously, if you are prone to cussing or belching or scratching your genitals when alone, restrain yourself and exhibit discernment regarding certain private behaviors. Otherwise, be you in a manner appropriate to the moment. There is only one you in the entire world. Rejoice in your uniqueness and relax with who you are. Don't take on "false airs" thinking it will endear you to certain individuals. They will sense it, and you will come off as being fake or phony and unworthy of trust. Just be you. How easy is that?

KEY POINTS

- ➤ Wisdom is the appropriate use of knowledge.
- ➤ Never pretend to have knowledge without certainty.
- ➤ Be yourself. There is only one you in the entire world.

CHAPTER 3

Communication Bytes, but It's What It Is

> ➤ Electronic conversation is the future of selling.
> ➤ Shorten all e-mails for time-compressed customers.
> ➤ We live in a world of educational bytes.
> ➤ Do not resist change.
> ➤ Constantly strive to develop new skills and techniques.

The Fragmented Presentations of Today

Historically, the consumer used to walk into your store, gallery, shop, or retail outlet. In 2004, 50 percent of the customers walked into a retail outlet, 40 percent called on the phone initially, and 10 percent made contact via the Internet. The benefit of the consumer coming to us was that it allowed for trust to be created quickly, especially coupled with brand recognition of your product. The product you were selling had physical attributes that allowed for the sales professional to capitalize on the uniqueness of the product, the urgency of the specific inventory on the floor, or a potential price increase due to a store sale ending. Consumers were able to touch/taste/

see/smell/feel all of this when they walked through your front door.

Presently, however, consumers do a majority of their gathering of information through the Internet and perhaps some phone conversations. They are much less likely to walk through your front door. As a matter of fact, the probability is that 85 percent of the leads that come into your company start from the Internet and phone. Subsequently, the ability to capitalize on walk-in traffic has diminished drastically over the past five years while the use of technology for the customer's due diligence has increased exponentially.

As a result, our ability to capitalize on e-mail and phone leads has also increased substantially!

It is important that you identify the changes in your presentation dynamics to assist you in restructuring your sales presentation. In today's world, a high-end product presentation seldom happens in one meeting. It could take numerous conversations ranging from several days to several months to get a definitive buying choice. Sales professionals must pace themselves and structure the presentation accordingly. A true sales athlete must realize that he cannot typically close a transaction on the first conversation. Understand that first and foremost and you can start to create an improved fragmented sales presentation based on fundamental practices that can seamlessly be applied to the present-day sales environment and to the product being represented.

As we discussed, the sales presentation today is highly fragmented and revolves around numerous e-mails, phone conversations, and various mail and collateral pieces and rarely results in a face-to-face meeting. By properly layering the presentation and systematically creating a "next step," a fragmented presentation can appear to be seamless, and an unspoiled presentation employing all the sales fundamentals can be delivered.

By using a next-step philosophy, your prospect is allowed to go through "gates" that consciously and subconsciously get that customer closer and closer to making an informed decision. There are key indicators that they have passed through these gates, are progressing further, and are taking possession of your product. Knowing and understanding time constraints and the amount of information a person can absorb during each portion of the fragmented presentation is critical to how you segment your presentation.

> *The first half-dozen e-mails to a customer should be no longer than four sentences. The last sentence must be a simple question that is easy to answer and commands a response.*

The Dos and Deaths of E-mail

There are many factors that go into improving one's ability to converse electronically. Consumers have shifted from visiting a sales center or going to a service company to gain information to obtaining the same information electronically. They usually search for multiple products before they make any selection of what product makes sense to them. It is at that time that the consumer reaches out and contacts a firm—when they are very well versed in the product and the competitor's products. An enticing website is necessary to engage the consumer from just being curious and move him in the direction of becoming interested. In today's market, the sales professional has to make the connection regarding how to take a slightly interested consumer and advance that consumer into wanting to actually buy a particular product strictly by using electronic conversation. The constant mistakes in this process can be easily diagnosed, but the strategy to fix these mistakes needs to be carefully crafted and executed.

The following is a series of dos and don'ts that can be applied to electronic conversation for the sales professional.

> If a customer has inquired via e-mail, reply via e-mail. Don't pick up the phone and call him. The customer has given you a clue that he prefers to converse electronically.

> Do not respond immediately when you receive a response to your initial e-mail. Whatever the time from when you sent your initial e-mail to when you receive an initial response, the follow-up e-mail should have a 50 percent wait factor; that is, if the customer took six hours to respond, your response should be in three hours.

> The first half-dozen e-mails should be no longer than four sentences. And the last sentence must be a simple question that is easy to answer and commands a response, thus keeping the conversation moving.

> The first e-mail cannot—repeat, cannot—have any attachments or PDF files.

> The first e-mail can have an image imbedded into the e-mail, but, again, not as an attachment.

> If the lead has come through the Internet, at no time should the sales professional ask if he can call the customer on the phone. That invitation to call only comes from the customer asking the sales professional to call him.

> Do not be confrontational; be friendly. Use the customer's words and verbiage in the beginning, and avoid industry-specific terms and acronyms.

> Success may simply be when the customer asks you to call him on the phone as opposed to continuing e-mail.

> In today's market, the sales professional has to make the connection regarding how to take a slightly interested consumer and advance that consumer into wanting to actually buy a particular product strictly by using electronic conversation.

Ignorance of these guidelines can result in the typical mistakes that sales professionals unknowingly and repeatedly make that not only burn through expensive leads but more importantly cause the consumer to go to a competitor; you may never be able to retrieve the opportunity again. You blew it!

The following are some basic guidelines of things to do when a customer inquires about your product/company electronically:

- ➢ Respond electronically.
- ➢ Keep your first three responses very brief.
- ➢ Ask a question at the end of each e-mail.
- ➢ Visualize a face-to-face conversation as you construct your e-mails.
- ➢ Be patient, and allow the conversation to develop into a deeper level of interest and understanding.
- ➢ Use the 50 percent wait factor in between e-mails. If the customer took six hours to respond, your response should be in three hours.
- ➢ Have the next three e-mails already prepared and well written to allow for a directed conversation to develop.
- ➢ Be flexible if the conversation goes off course according to your prepared e-mails, but make slight adjustments if need be and get your strategy back on course as quickly as possible.

> ➤ Always ask yourself, *Why did I say this? Why did I ask this question? Did I ask the right question? Did I anticipate this response?* (much more to come on this)
> ➤ Monitor the responses and see if there are any patterns to the pace of the conversation, and also note the level of detailed questions that are being asked.

The War and Peace E-mail Syndrome

In this specific case, a team of sales professionals received web-based inquiries about their product. They were all using the same canned two-page e-mail response, trying to cover every aspect of the product and hoping that something in the e-mail would appeal to the new lead. I will refer to this as the *War and Peace* e-mail—a painfully long e-mail that many will not read. You remember Tolstoy's *War and Peace*, a very, very long and thick book. The consumer response to the initial e-mail was less than 1 percent. The estimated cost of each lead was $750, including the creative work, the media cost of the ad, and the staffing hours to receive the lead and transfer it to the sales professional. Additionally, these leads were inbound, meaning that the customer was curious enough to send an e-mail requesting more information. Of the thousand leads that came in, nine hundred were responded to in the typical way, a long-winded *War and Peace* type e-mail of meaningless detail; meaningless because the sales professional had no personal information on what the customer was exactly interested in. These initial e-mails resulted in a 1 percent response of nine leads that responded and wanted even more information. From that 1 percent response there was only one transaction. The remaining hundred leads were sent a series of well-crafted, short e-mails that basically thanked them for their interest and asked how the sales professional could assist them. From this effort, there was a 30 percent response; thirty people wanted to learn more. They went from curious to interested. And through the practices that are taught in this book and at training seminars, the electronic conversation ultimately ended up with a result of a 20 percent close, or a total of six transactions.

Let's analyze each program. The specific costs and results were as follows:

Program 1—*War and Peace*
900 leads @ $750/lead = $675,000
1 transaction = $250,000
Closing % = 0.1%
Monetary efficiency = $0.37/lead
Basically you will go broke with this type of strategy.

Program 2—Optimum Efficiency
100 leads @$750/lead = $75,000
6 transactions @ $250,000 per transaction = $1,500,000
Closing % = 6.0%
Monetary efficiency = $20.00/lead
You can grow a company with this type of response.

Here is one more interesting statistic. Of the 891 leads that never got a response (900 leads less the 9 responses), the new strategic short e-mail communication plan was used at a later date to try to recapture these wasted leads. A 10 percent response was recorded with 92 responses; the same lead, within six months of the original e-mail, and 90+ raised their hand wanting to learn more. From the 92 that responded, nearly a 9 percent close was realized, resulting in revenues of $2,000,000.

This is the analysis of the recapture effort:

891 leads at no cost due to the fact that these leads had already been paid for
8 transactions @ $250,000 per transaction = $2,000,000
Closing percentage 8.98%

Monetary efficiency = $2,245/lead

It may be time you look at how you are communicating with your customers.

Be critical of your current situation and make changes quickly!

So what is wrong with your company, your sales staff, your reps, your personal performance, your business, and your services? Ask yourself: *Why don't my clients want to talk to me? What am I doing wrong? And most importantly, how do I fix this?*

As humans, we become comfortable with our current situation. Maybe you have had some success doing things a certain way in the past, but they just don't seem to be working anymore. Maybe it is just because you are scared to try something new, even though it is proven and effective, because it may not work for you. Or possibly, up until now, you just didn't know how to get started.

KEY POINTS

> - Due to technology, the very nature of communication has shifted radically from just ten years ago.
> - In e-mails, way less is so much more.
> - E-mail, Facebook, tweets, and twitters have shaped the way we communicate today.
> - If you are still communicating as a sales professional the way you did a decade ago, you are resisting change, stagnating, and losing potential income.
> - Just like a top athlete, sales athletes must constantly push themselves to learn and develop new skills and techniques to stay on top of their game.

Maybe you have had some success doing things a certain way in the past but they just don't seem to be working anymore. Maybe it is just because you are scared to try something new, even though it is proven and effective, because it may not work for you.

CHAPTER 4

The Universal Laws of E-mail

> ➤ There are universal laws of e-mail that cannot be ignored.
> ➤ Create short, efficient, well-crafted e-mails.

These are universal statistics about e-mail: 80 percent of people will read an e-mail if it is less than four sentences. Conversely, only 20 percent will read an e-mail longer than four sentences. And only 5 percent of people will read an e-mail over two paragraphs. If you are trying to get to the largest number of people possible, don't fight it; just make your e-mails no more than four sentences. Additionally, a very high percentage of people who read these short e-mails will respond if the last sentence is an easy-to-answer question. It is highly recommended that the question can simply be answered by the word "yes."

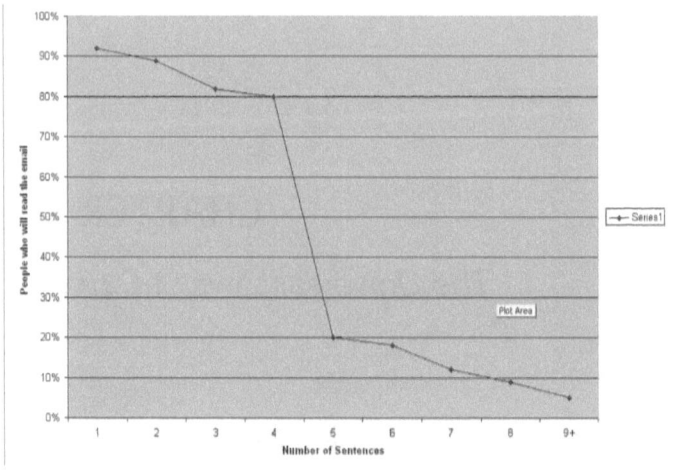

Have a strategy before each and every customer encounter, interaction, and meeting utilizing the sales fundamentals. Start with customers whom you have never met. Start with a plan that provides a platform for the next three e-mails. From the first e-mail to the next, for these three first encounters you should simply bear in mind that you need to modify your current presentation so that each e-mail complements the other, creating a seamless order. The goal for the first e-mail is to simply thank them for contacting you and then ask a *simple* question. The intent is simply to start a conversation, in this case electronically. Similar to an interactive conversation in person, the goal is to have it go back and forth to allow for both parties to chat.

> *80 percent of people will read an e-mail if it is less than four sentences.*

Strategically Concise E-mailing: No More Than Four Sentences

Thank you stopping by our booth and for your interest in ACME PREOWNED VEHICLES. Were you interested in the newest arrivals on our lot, or in a specific make and model?

This type of question is a choice question. It is also assumptive in nature. It is not asking *if* they were interested. It assumes that they were interested in one of the two preowned vehicles. Secondly, it is asking a question and demanding a response. The follow-up e-mail, regardless of their response to you, would be as follows:

ACME PREOWNED VEHICLES is a "no dickering/no negotiating" dealership. Prices start at X, while allowing our new owners to take home vehicles that are valued at 50 percent to 100 percent more at other dealerships. Is this the type of car dealership you were looking for?

In this case it's two sentences and a question. Again, regardless of their answer, e-mail number three is:

Thank you for your response. As you might guess, ACME PREOWNED VEHICLES is not designed for everyone. However, our current owners tell us that they knew very early if they liked our sales concept or not. Can you tell me how often you have been to our nationwide dealerships?

If you combine all three, you can dissect that you are doing some meet and greet, a little warm up, a mild intent statement, a member statement, and a takeaway. In addition you have transitioned into discovery by asking a discovery question. To try to achieve this in one e-mail would be ludicrous and nonproductive. You may not even get a response. Start any electronic conversation as you would an oral conversation.

Forecast, stage, and end presentations at a time when it maximizes positive and key points. A strategic sales presentation is surgical in extracting the information you need quickly and efficiently. However, it is never rushed. If you are having a conversation and the customer has requested a collateral item such as a brochure or an article about your product, tell them that you will send it to him after you hang up, but ask a few more relevant questions.

For example, if a customer asks, "How do you arrive at the prices on your cars?" then your answer should be, "I will e-mail you an overview of how we trade, but may I ask what type of vehicle are you looking for?" If there are kids involved, ask, "Do the kids travel with you in this vehicle? Or would this be strictly a work vehicle?"

You could have answered the customer's question directly. That's the knowledge they seek. But then where would you go (lack of wisdom)?

By answering their question with your question, you now have a slightly deeper level of understanding as to the personal needs of your customer. Assume nothing, and ask the question. Now that you have the answers to your questions, you could potentially answer the same request for how you arrive at your pricing as follows:

> Since your kids might be with you sometimes, but mostly the vehicle will be used for work, I would recommend that you take a look at these two similar yet quite different makes and models. One of my recent owners went with a slightly larger rig for greater durability.

You now have a constructive conversation on makes and sizes *and* you have gained knowledge through a couple of simple discovery questions that can set up the next conversation or the next step. By design, you do *not* send the brochure on the larger rig, which strategically provides you a reason to reconnect later if you don't get a response.

Use positioning statements through a customer statement: "You sound like most of our customers."—**Wisdom**

Future pace their response. This means you will tell them how they will feel about what you are going to say and you anticipate another contact: "You will love this next feature, and there may only be a couple of other questions to see if you think owning one of these will work for you and the family ... let me ask you this ..."—**Wisdom**

You know you must ask for the order ... just be certain to ask at the right time.—**Wisdom**

Lead into closing with trial closes and positioning statements. Be prepared if they say yes; be prepared if feeling resistance or time boxed.—**Knowledge and Wisdom**

Always ask a question in your follow-up e-mail if you want a response. Asking a question triggers a need to respond. If your previous conversation included a leading response, the question should be relevant and should continue the conversation: "I forgot to make note of whether your wife will also be driving this vehicle."

Ask the question even if you know the answer, as it continues the conversation. It also positions you for more questions, such as, "Do you ever go off-road?" or "What kind of driving would your wife do with this vehicle?" or "Exactly how often would this vehicle be for your hunting use?"

The knowledge is that they play, drive, and hunt. The wisdom you can impart to them is gained by drilling down and discovering what kind of use they envision for their vehicle. Do they like to play together? Where would they like to go? You do these things to make the key drivers of your product relevant to them and to develop those features.

KEY POINTS

- ➢ E-mails should have no more than four sentences, and the last sentence must be a simple question.
- ➢ Develop a logical sequence of e-mails with relevant questions.

CHAPTER 5

Developing an E-mail Strategy—
Were They Dead Leads or
Did You Just Kill Them?

> ➤ Start now with a self-diagnosis!
> ➤ Develop a new e-mail strategy.
> ➤ Time compression in everyone's life requires short, efficient e-mails.

Most salespeople find through self-analysis that they have no strategy at all, just an initial universal e-mail that was ineffective at getting a response.

The following is an exercise that will begin the process of how to converse effectively through e-mails or text.

> ➤ Print the last twenty e-mail chains that you have sent. Separate those that did not get a response from those that did.
> ➤ Assemble each series of e-mails in chronological order.

> ➢ Note the length of the e-mails. If they look long, then they are, and you have appealed to a maximum of 20 percent of those you have sent them to.
> ➢ Don't worry; they're not dead yet. You could still revive 80 percent of them!
> ➢ Assuming they did respond, what was the content of your second e-mail? Was it too long?
> ➢ Was the last sentence a question?
> ➢ Was the question easy to answer with yes, no, or a one-word response?
> ➢ What was the purpose of the question? Random questions are meaningless. Ask questions that tell you more about the customer and provide critical information.
> ➢ What was the strategy of your communication plan?

Most people find through self-analysis that they have no strategy at all, just an initial universal e-mail that was ineffective at getting a response. And if by chance there was a response by a customer, they really had no clue what to do next, because there was not a communication plan in place. So any adjustment in this area will create immediate and positive changes.

It is as important to recognize *what not* to do, as it is to know *what* to do. It is important to be realistic and highly critical at this point. Here are the next steps in turning your business around through electronic conversation. Typically, people experience a 100 percent improvement in the number of responses by making a few simple changes to their initial e-mail. Much higher numbers are anticipated as you perfect the skills of a strategic e-mail communication plan and experiment with what creates the highest results for your particular situation.

Start from the beginning. One of the major goals of the e-mail campaign should include simply trying to establish an electronic conversation. Just as in a face-to-face conversation with a person you have just met, the best conversations flow back and forth, with both parties being involved in the conversation, and develop quickly because they are inspired by asking questions. Since you don't know much or anything about this person, you begin by asking simple, noninvasive questions. As you get to know the person better, you can lengthen the conversation as well as the level and depth of questions.

The recommended goal is to craft e-mails that position you for the next four or five conversational interactions, all with questions such that when the client responds, you can reply with information that helps you develop a better understanding of what their needs might be, establishes a better relationship through the development of a meaningful conversation, and assists the customer in gaining information and trust in you.

KEY POINTS

- ➤ Examine what your e-mails have been like up to now. Be brutally honest.
- ➤ Constantly monitor and revise your e-mails for optimum results.
- ➤ Less truly is more.

CHAPTER 6

Physics and Sales

The Science of Selling

- ➢ There are some correlations between human behavior and physical laws.
- ➢ Sales athletes must act as catalysts to initiate action.
- ➢ Love is a powerful motivational force.
- ➢ Diversions, such as surfing the web, can be devastating to your personal goals.
- ➢ People tend to resist taking action (fear) until another more powerful force overrides their disposition (need).

The laws of physics sometimes apply to human behavior, and none more so than Newton's Laws of Motion, especially those regarding inertia and action.

1. Every object persists in its state of rest or uniform motion in a straight line, unless it is compelled to change that state by forces impressed upon it.
2. For every action, there is an equal and opposite reaction.

Let's examine number one. Have you ever noticed that even if you want your child to clean his or her room, want your customer to buy your product, want your husband to watch something other than the same network news show he always watches, want your friend to try another restaurant rather than the same old, same old, even though *you want those things*, nothing seems to change unless you somehow impact the situation?

Our customers are hard-wired by the laws of inertia. They are predisposed to do nothing differently than they have done before. They would rather "think about it" than *do something* about it.

Your child would much prefer to think about cleaning his or her room than actually clean the room. Thinking is much easier and far more comfortable than doing.

> *Our customers are hard-wired by the laws of inertia. They are predisposed to do nothing different than they have done before. They would rather "think about it" than do something about it.*

Now let's look at that second point: "For every action there is an equal and opposite reaction."

How does it feel when your friend, wife, husband, boss, child—whomever—"tells you" what you should do next? Do you ever feel resistant to their "suggestions" or demands?

Of course you do. We all do, because for every action there is an equal and opposite reaction. It is quite simply a tug-of-war. We pull them, and they pull away from us. In romance, why do we always chase the ones who run away? Why do we want the ones who are hard to get? Why does no one want to belong to a club that wants them as a member? The human dynamic is subject to Newtonian Laws of Motion.

So how do we as sales athletes impress change upon bodies in states of rest without causing them to react oppositely from our desired goals? Tricky, isn't it?

Telling our customers what to do is only effective when they were already predisposed to have taken our suggested course before they ever met us. That is affectionately called "a lay down." We all get those. It does not indicate any measure of talent. It merely indicates that the salesperson was in the right place at exactly the right moment.

> *Talent is exemplified by those individuals who can motivate "a body at rest" that has no predisposition to do what you would like it to do.*

Let's go back to the child and the messy room.

As a parent "selling" your child on organizing the chaos in his or her room, you can threaten, cajole, or plead. The first two involve fear tactics. The latter involves a guilt tactic. You can scream really loud! That too is a fear tactic. We have all seen, experienced, or heard sales techniques of those varieties. The technique is called "fear of loss."

You could tell your child, "I happen to know for a fact that there is a $5 bill hidden somewhere in this mess. Perhaps if you organize your room, you will find it!"

Now your child (customer) is no longer afraid of *not* cleaning the room but rather is selfishly motivated in hopes of finding some personal gain hidden within their mess.

That's called "hope for gain."

Or you could employ both techniques via yelling too loudly that there will either be a punishment incurred for nonactivity *or* a possible profit via taking action now and cleaning.

That is called "fear of loss and hope for gain," a tactic that is commonly employed by many marketers and salespeople. Think of all those infomercials we have all seen.

Does it work? Sure it does. Is it common? Yes, it is so common it stinks of mediocrity.

These are common tactics that can facilitate and enable motion in bodies at rest. They are also overused to the point of causing an equal and opposite reaction. As such, they are only preliminarily effective.

It is simply remarkable how people will bend over backward to please you if they sense—genuinely sense—that you genuinely care about them, that you love them.

"Success leaves clues." This is the "clue" left behind by truly talented, exceptionally great sales athletes. Their customers buy from them because of *them*! Their customers have an almost uncanny desire to want to please their salesperson. Sure, the product has something to do with it. But really, nobody actually needs most of the things we sell from day to day.

Our friends do not *need* to try the new tavern down the block. Our spouses do not *need* to mow the lawn, paint the fence, go shopping, see a movie, or try a particular diet. Our customers do not really *need* our product as opposed to another similar product. In fact, do they really *need* what we have at all?

We want them to want what we want them to want! That is what selling is about. While there are many tricks and sales tactics to achieve those ends, the most effective way to affect someone's desire is by loving them to the point of gaining their implicit trust and desire to please us. They buy what we sell because of *us*—because we love them, and they love that! Really, selling can be a veritable love fest! And if it isn't that way for you right now, then you had best start working on the concept of why it is you sell!

One final note about Newton's Laws of Motion and sales: an object that is in motion will not change its velocity unless an *unbalanced force* acts upon it.

Translated, that means "Don't talk past the close." We all do it. We are chatting with our significant other, passionately and emphatically making the point we want to be making. The poor person listening has already agreed with us more than once, and yet we carry on, making the point and wallowing in the sound of our own voices.

Stop! Do *not* be the "unbalanced force."

Sometimes we can be our own worst enemies. When your customer, friend, child, or spouse is ready for the next step, go to the next step. Stop talking! Get out of the way of the momentum you have created. Great sales athletes know that silence is golden. Get out of the way and move forward!

Wow, I bet Mr. Newton could have been one helluva sales athlete! Of course we have all bought into his theories, so maybe he was!

> *It is simply remarkable how people will bend over backward to please you if they sense—genuinely sense—that you sincerely care about them, that you love them.*

Newton's Interpretation of the Coefficient of Friction

According to Newton, friction is "the resistance an object encounters in moving over another."

In this case, the resistance for individuals to make changes to their existing habits has a resistive force. What does it take to make an individual make changes? Some changes are easier than others.

It is easier to drag an object over glass than over sandpaper. The reason for this is that the sandpaper exerts more frictional resistance. In many problems, it is assumed that a surface is "smooth," which means that it does not exert any frictional force. In real life, however, this wouldn't be the case. Life always offers us "rough" surfaces that will offer "frictional resistance."

Some people can make changes easily, and their change is a relatively smooth transition. Others resist change and can resist change so much that it is tragically detrimental—and by the time they make changes, they have completely missed the opportunities at hand or are out of business. What type of person are you? Do you resist change?

Limiting Equilibrium

Imagine that you are trying to push a book along a table with your finger. If you apply only a very small force, the book will not move. This must mean that the frictional force is equal to the force with which you are pushing the book. If the frictional force were less than the force produced by your finger, the book would slide forward.

If the frictional force was greater you could push the book a bit harder, but it would still remain stationary. The frictional force must therefore have increased, or the book would have moved. If you continue to push harder, eventually a point is reached when the frictional force increases no more. When the frictional force is at its maximum possible value, friction is said to be *limiting*. If friction is limiting yet the book is still stationary, it is said to be in *limiting equilibrium*. If you push ever so slightly harder, the book will start to move. If the body is now moving, friction will be taking its *limiting value*.

Our delicate job as salespeople is to find the limiting value required to get your clients moving in the direction you desire them to be moving without exhibiting too much force so as to cause their resistance to your suggestions. It is always best if the customer believes it is his idea to move forward.

Goofing Off—A Limiting Equilibrium?

One significant downside of today's technology is the impact the Internet can have on our own momentum at work. The Internet supplies us with a "frictional force" that can negatively impact our forward momentum. We have all done it. We are all guilty to some degree. Information is so readily available to our fingertips that the temptation is nearly irresistible.

How did the stock market perform today? Where can I order periwinkles for my next dinner soirée? What has Lindsay Lohan done this time? How many angels actually do fit on the head of a pin?

Anything we want to know, we can find out in a few seconds. The trouble is that every time we do that we are coming to a dead standstill in our work (limiting equilibrium), which in turn will require some amount of energy to get going again (limiting value) against the "limiting friction" of digression.

> *It is so important to maintain a level of professionalism and self-discipline while working and to not fall prey to the temptations of Googling, checking Facebook, tweeting and texting, or otherwise surfing the web or goofing off. The time wasted can never be gotten back, and the momentum lost could be cumulatively devastating to the accomplishment of our goals. Save your idle meanderings for after-work hours.*

In Summary

The frictional force between two objects is not constant but increases until it reaches a maximum value. When the frictional force is at its maximum, the body in question will either be moving or will be on the verge of moving.

Are you close to making changes? Have you experienced so much resistance from yourself, clients, business partners, or government officials that you have limited your ability to be successful? What will it take for you to actually make changes and put the necessary effort into being successful? But more than anything, why do you resist change if your current selling techniques have proven themselves to cause you to fall short of your desired goals?

KEY POINTS

- ➤ We are all subject to certain Newtonian laws.
- ➤ Inertia is a powerful force that can only be affected by an outside stimulus.
- ➤ Fear of loss is powerful; hope for gain is more powerful; and love is the greatest motivational force of all.
- ➤ Avoid the limiting factors of digression while working.
- ➤ It is natural for all of us to resist change until a greater desire overcomes the "limiting friction" factor.

CHAPTER 7

The HeART of Selling

➤ Acting is not pretending.
➤ The intent and quality of your actions is not dictated by voice or movement.
➤ Appropriate (truthful) action is based entirely upon the spontaneity of the moment as it exists.
➤ Great selling is a function of love.
➤ True power in communication is based upon the "quality of intent" within you and your ability to focus that intent toward another.

The Secret Sauce

Let's examine something a little more tangible. Let's talk about actors and acting. What does "acting" mean?

What does it mean for an actor to act? Simply stated, it means "to take an action" and nothing more. So if it is as simple as that, what makes a great actor great and everyone else somewhere between good and terrible? What does it mean "to take an action"? Does that mean running around waving your arms? Does it mean putting on wigs and costumes while talking loudly or laughing wildly? What does it mean "to take action"?

When was the last time you watched someone on a soap opera or daytime TV or caught a few minutes of any Disney Channel program? By chance did you happen to notice how "bad" that acting actually is? The great acting coach Harold Guskin likens bad actors to Martians talking to each other. Everything they do seems out of adjustment to the circumstances of the moment; they are not taking believable actions.

So just exactly what is the secret sauce?

> *Greatness has little to do with rehearsed and preconceived notions of what is important to the task at hand. That would be the definition of good or mediocrity. Greatness is the result of quality of intent, vulnerability, razor-like focus, and emotional availability to the task at hand in the specific moment!*

The Tonight Show with Johnny Carson

In the old days of *The Tonight Show*, Johnny Carson was the host. His guest one evening was the preeminent British actor Lord Laurence Olivier. Olivier was quite old at the time. He'd already been honored by the Queen with knighthood and then later made a national treasure by receiving a lordship from Her Majesty. Olivier was arguably one of the very finest actors of modern times, reigning over all his peers in both live theater and cinematic performance.

He and Carson were chatting casually about his recent film release, *The Boys from Brazil*. Their conversation was quite subdued, as you might imagine a conversation to be with an elderly and distinguished British lord.

In mid-conversation, Carson politely asked Lord Olivier if he would be so kind as to recite some Shakespeare for the audience.

"What do you have in mind?" Lord Olivier asked.

"Uh, I don't know. Whatever you like; something brief, like maybe a poem," Carson responded.

"Very well; we'll keep it simple. How about a very brief sonnet?" With that, Lord Olivier went to work.

The only weird thing is that he didn't do anything. He didn't have any props. In fact all that happened was this:

He leaned forward ever so slightly in his chair to get comfortable toward the camera, which zoomed in on his face. Resting his elbow on one knee, he recited a sixteen-line Shakespearean love sonnet in a very quiet and monotone voice. He did not raise an eyebrow. He did not move a muscle on his face. Sixteen short lines, and he was done.

When he finished, there was absolute stunned silence in the live audience, a long, very uncomfortable kind of silence as the television camera panned back to a full shot of the set.

Then, suddenly, the live theater audience was up on its feet applauding hysterically, as if they could not clap their hands hard enough. They whistled, hollered "Bravo," and cheered with all their might. Johnny Carson was in tears, literally wiping them away as he too applauded on his feet this great actor's moment.

And here is the strangest part of all. I was ten years old at the time and had been granted a late night to watch TV with my dad. I knew nothing about love, Shakespeare's sonnets (other than that I couldn't understand a word of it), or acting. All I knew was that I had "goose flesh" on my arms, and as I looked over at my father, who was a lower-middle-class factory worker for his entire life, he too, just like Carson, had tears welling up in his eyes. I remember asking, "Dad, what happened?" My father could not respond. He was too choked up and embarrassed. He just shrugged.

All this hard, deep, emotional reaction came from a simple sixteen-line poem, done with nothing other than a calm, monotone voice that was sent via an electronic signal of Olivier's face across the continent into the cathodes and tubes of our family's ancient black-and-white television set. My father and I were just as moved, by virtually nothing, as was the live TV audience in the New York sound stage of *The Tonight Show.*

Quality of Intent, Vulnerability, Razor-Like Focus, and Emotional Availability

And so here I am now, to repeat that same profound question: "What happened?"

What Olivier did, as have so many other greats such as Michael Jordan, Dustin Hoffman, Meryl Streep, Nelson Mandela, Coach Wooden, Tiger Woods, Gandhi, and Mother Teresa, to name a mere few, was to possess and be able to command "quality of intent" via refined mental and physical discipline to the desired purpose.

What was the "quality of intent" Olivier was projecting that night? Here was an old man on *The Tonight Show* promoting his most recent film. Perhaps he was tired that night or suffering from arthritis. Perhaps he just ate a big meal and had terrible gas and was experiencing bloating. Perhaps he would have much rather been at home in England sitting in front of his TV watching a good soccer match. However, in that less than a minute, with a sixteen-line sonnet, regardless of his human weaknesses, aged frailty, vulnerabilities, and distractions, he summoned his professionalism, training, and focus to project a man madly, deeply in love—so much so that we were all infected with his projection and "bought it" hook, line, and sinker!

In these superlative artisans of their unique crafts, the "fire burns hot." It is their additional one degree of heat that makes the water in them boil. That is the difference between good and great!

Look at what happened to Tiger Woods, who rated so much lower among top golfers after his personal upsets. Was he not the same man he was before? He may even have the same swing. What happened to him? As Gary Player once stated about the game of golf, "We create success or failure on the course primarily by our thoughts."

Greatness has little to do with rehearsed and preconceived notions of what is important to the task at hand. That would be the definition of good or mediocrity. Greatness is the result of quality of intent, vulnerability, razor-like focus, and emotional availability to the task at hand in the specific moment!

As sales athletes, your fire must also burn hot. In the case of selling today, the projections you must rouse within yourself have to do with "love" in varying degrees.

> *If love can move mountains, then it most certainly can make a sale.*

Selling as a Function of Love

So what is the most effective way of impressing a stimulus upon a body at rest without causing "push back," resentment, lack of trust, and/or lack of credibility? Who is immune to being cared for and/or genuinely being cared about? No one is immune to love.

There is a song in the musical play *Camelot* by Lerner and Lowe called "How to Handle a Woman." If I were to rewrite those lyrics, they would look like this.

Do I threaten or cajole or plead?
Do I brood or play the gay romancer?
Said he smiling, "No indeed."

How to handle a client
"There's a way," said the wise old man.
"The way to handle a client is to love them.
Simply love them.

Merely love them.
Love them. Love them."

That song would be called "How to Handle a Client," or better still "How to Handle Everyone"! Merely love them, love them, love them!

We submit, as we have done and will do repeatedly throughout this book, that the best way to

> ➢ get a child to clean his room, get good grades, or do anything, for that matter;
> ➢ get your spouse to go to dinner or a dance with you;
> ➢ get your employees motivated and activated;
> ➢ get your friends to go to your favorite restaurant or to try a particular hike that you enjoy; or
> ➢ get *your customers to buy* ...

... is to love them. They can sense that, and love is powerful magic.

Think about it for just a moment. Why do we sell to others? Why do we want someone to try our favorite new restaurant? Why do we implore a friend or family member to see the game with us? Why do we coerce someone special to us to try out our new exercise routine? Why do we work hard to convince our children to develop good habits?

Isn't it because we love them? Extrapolating the concept forward, don't we sales athletes sell products that we believe in and share them with our customers, because (no matter how removed the concept) we love them?

You may say that it is because that is how we make a living! However, I submit that if you sell your product to whomever just to make money, you will never be great at selling.

In his book, *The Spirit to Serve*, J. W. Marriott proposes quite astutely that business success is based upon a spirit of service.

Translated, that means that business success must be based upon a foundation of love and genuine caring.

> *Great sales athletes will choose to "love" their customers via serving their needs with the product! In doing so, the "money" will follow as a by-product of their great service.*

KEY POINTS

➤ Acting is taking a truthful action appropriate to the moment to create the desired result.

➤ The power of your actions is controlled by emotional content and not by physical activity.

➤ To be perceived as being truthful, the actions you take and the communications you put forth must be based upon the moment itself, your desired outcome, and being emotionally available to those two items.

➤ Great selling is a function of love, service, and genuine caring.

➤ Once you discern the true needs of the moment, use disciplined focus and emotional availability to achieve your desired result. That is true communication power used by the finest actors ... or those who take actions!

CHAPTER 8

You Manifest What You Are

> ➤ What you believe dictates your reality
> ➤ Do, Have, Be or Be, Do, Have? That is the question.
> ➤ What goes on between your ears is all that counts.

You Are What You Manifest

Most of the Western world believes that the following is the order of reality. To achieve, one must first *DO* what an athlete, musician, painter, business person, or parent does. Then you will *HAVE* what they have: children, art supplies, the right gear, business cards and customers, instruments, and music compositions. And finally, you will *BE* who you are.

Sadly, nothing could be further from the truth. Can you recall what all motivational books talk about almost without exception? What is *The Secret* all about? What did the good witch sing to Dorothy in the musical *The Wiz?* And for that matter, what did the Wizard of Oz give to the Scarecrow, the Tin Man, and the Cowardly Lion?

It all starts with *BElief* in oneself and one's goals. To become, to realize, to manifest, to create starts with *BEing.*

Eastern philosophers know this. The actual order of human reality is:

BE—DO—HAVE

In your consciousness you must *BElieve* deeply in your dreams and desires. Then you must "take action" and *DO* to create momentum toward those goals, and finally, with time and hard work, your dreams and desires will manifest and you will *HAVE* what you wanted. Just be careful what you wish for.

One of the biggest-selling "success" books over the last seventy years is Napoleon Hill's *Think and Grow Rich*. In it he expresses the basic tenant "What the mind of a man can conceive and believe can be achieved."

So what do actors, the recitation of Shakespearian love sonnets, and success philosophies have to do with sales? *First, believing!* Remember when we were children how we would *make believe?* Now, as adults, *believe* with all your might!

Start everything with *BElief. BE* a successful salesperson. *BE* in control. *BE* love. *BE* healthy. *BE* genuinely caring. *BE* confident. *BE* still within in the midst of chaos. *BE* the best salesperson in the universe. *BE* courage. *BE* strength. "Don't worry. *BE* happy." What you are *BEing* is what your customer will "pick up on" far more than anything you do or what you have to sell them.

Think of a ten-year class reunion. You have probably been amazed at how some of your old classmates have changed—the "geek" who now runs a large corporation, the "ugly Betty" who is now a TV star, the handsome football star who is now a big fat loser, or the shy kid who is now a great defense attorney. How did these changes occur? You saw them as you thought they were. They saw themselves as they believed they would be. By believing in themselves they learned to behave and act like the vision they held within.

Their transformations took time; there were changes that are barely visible to those who saw them every day. However, to everyone else who hasn't seen them in ten years, the transformation seems almost unbelievable!

Ralph Waldo Emerson said, "What lies behind us and what lies before us are tiny matters compared to what lies within us." Change your thoughts and beliefs; change your life!

> *"Remember, whether you think you can or cannot accomplish a goal—either way, you're right!"—Henry Ford. Be cautious of the chatter inside your mind and what you are setting up for yourself as a belief.*

KEY POINTS

> ➢ It is easy to perceive the steps of manifestation backward: HAVE; DO; BE.
> ➢ BE in your mind who you want to be.
> ➢ DO what must be done to achieve your dreams and desires.
> ➢ HAVE is the end result of BE and DO.

CHAPTER 9

The Undeniable and Critically Essential Sales Fundamentals

➤ Typically today's sales presentation is highly fragmented.
➤ There are six sales fundamentals.
➤ As a result of today's communication technologies and time-compressed customers, sales may not occur in a "linear order."
➤ Sales athletes must know their fundamentals inside-out and upside-down.
➤ Tension cannot exist when gaining trust and information.
➤ Tension must exist in order to make a sale.
➤ No shortcuts! Every segment is critical.

We will now begin to explore the process and key steps in identifying and/or creating needs in your customers that are aligned with your product's benefits as they relate to the customer's key value drivers. For our purposes, these steps will be referred to as the six sales fundamentals.

1. Meet/Greet/Warm Up (relating)
2. Intent Statements (sets the stage)

3. Discovery Questions (identifying/creating need)
4. Information Confirmation (building trust throughout the presentation by proving you are listening)
5. Feature/Benefit (advocating)
6. Close (the recommendation of action—always be closing)

While they are presented via a list in a specific order, it is critical to note that the order in which they may be used in actual practice will vary. The sales athlete must be disciplined and train constantly on the fundamentals in order to manifest a nimble and effortless demeanor regarding variations in the sequence of the six sales fundamentals based upon the infinite variables offered when interfacing with each specific customer type: drivers, amiables, expressives, analyticals, or any combination thereof.

Today's brief electronic communications with time-crunched customers makes it difficult to follow any "logical sequence" based on antiquated sales constructs of A through Z. The flow of the sales sequences today is based on the needs of our clients in a given moment and on their preferred method of communication when we finally are able to contact them.

It is critical to understand the sales process as a whole and not think of it any more as a linear progression of time, cause, and effect. A good analogy would be this: you understand the story line and overall themes of a film you have just seen from beginning to end via the movie projector; after the movie is over, that same linear projection, the entire film, is now sitting in its can up in the projection room. To deploy this high-level view of the six sales fundamentals, we will start with a metaphor to better understand the six sales fundamentals as a whole concept just like that film in its can.

The Sales Tree

The metaphor of a "sales tree" is made to assist in a high-level visualization of the varied components of sales fundamentals as a living entity for two reasons. First, each part of the tree (sales fundamentals) is dependent upon the other parts for the overall health (sales success) of the tree (sales presentation). Secondly, it is critical to always be aware of the sales fundamentals as an entire piece so you can know what you have already covered with your customer in your presentation and what remains yet to be covered.

> ➤ The *roots* represent *discovery* (all the nutrients/water needed for the tree and the tree's anchor upon which it can grow).
> ➤ The *trunk* represents *information confirmation* to be drip-fed back to the client when and where appropriate.
> ➤ The *big limbs* represent multiple *intent statements* (minor and major depending upon where you are in the sales process).
> ➤ The *small branches* represent the *features* of our products and how they will *benefit* the customer's many and diverse needs that we created/highlighted through questions (selling/advocating).
> ➤ The *leaves* represent *greeting* and *warm-up* (all the warm fuzzy feelings the tree gets from the sun through its leaves).
> ➤ The *fruit* represents *closing* the sale (the end result of our presentation).

It really does not matter which of the tree's parts are labeled to represent the six fundamentals. The whole point is to delineate what the six fundamentals are and to be cognizant of them via this metaphor.

More importantly, which part of the sales fundamentals could be skipped without "killing" the sales tree? When you trim steps (the leaves, branches, roots), your presentation downgrades into mediocrity depending upon how many steps you trim. Trim too many steps and you kill your sales presentation. Never trim your presentation and it will grow wild and ungainly and bear less fruit.

Now let's begin examining each sales fundamental in greater detail and determine why it is important to the tree.

Task Tension

For the purposes of persuasion, tension is a good thing. Remember Newton's Laws of Inertia and the Coefficient of Friction. It takes an outside force, energy, or pressure (tension) to get something to move and/or change direction.

The same is true in sales. No tension translates to no sale! If you want someone else to want to do what you want them to do (selling), you must do two things:

1. First lower task tension so that the person(s) you are working with will be able to trust, relax, and listen to you.
2. Next, deliberately raise task tension so that the same person(s) will be able to be "moved" to take the action of your predetermination!

The following graph shows what needs to be done and what actions are to be taken during the sales process to achieve your goal with the person to whom you are "selling."

> No tension translates to no sale!

Task Tension Graph

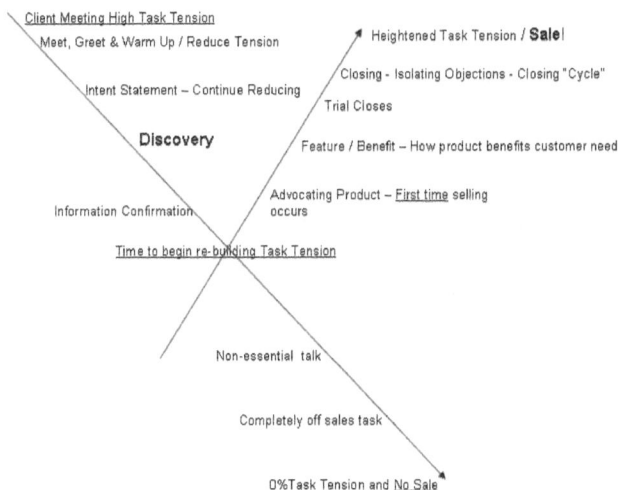

Client Meeting High Task Tension
Meet, Greet & Warm Up / Reduce Tension
Heightened Task Tension / **Sale**!
Closing - Isolating Objections - Closing "Cycle"
Intent Statement — Continue Reducing
Trial Closes
Discovery
Feature / Benefit — How product benefits customer need
Information Confirmation
Advocating Product — <u>First time</u> selling occurs
Time to begin re-building Task Tension
Non-essential talk
Completely off sales task
0%Task Tension and <u>No Sale</u>

Let's take an example: stubborn children. They don't want to clean their rooms, and you want them to. More so, you want them to *want to*. Of course you can force action through fear tactics, but that has a short-term gain.

You want to communicate with your child to get him to clean up his mess. First get him to relax around you. If you don't, yelling will be the next step—and a dead end.

How do you get him to relax? Easy—make some small talk. Ask him how his day was. Offer him a beverage. Ask him how he is feeling or tell him he looks great. Find out what he thought of that movie he saw yesterday, or how his friend is, or how the game went. You know—small talk. That is Meet/Greet and Warm Up.

Once you feel that he is feeling relaxed and not braced for possible confrontation, ask him some simple questions relevant to your end goal of cleaning the room. (Is any of this sounding familiar?)

1. Do you ever misplace things?
2. How does that make you feel?
3. Tell me about your favorite place you ever stayed.
4. How did it look?
5. Was it organized or messy, like your room?
6. How did that make you feel?
7. Do you ever feel like there is no time to get things done?
8. Do you ever get a task from a teacher that is so complex you wonder where to begin?
9. How does that make you feel?
10. What do you do when that happens? How do you begin such a big task?

That was a "Discovery." Then repeat back to your kid what he just said: "So let me see if I understand. Sometimes you do lose items and it makes you get upset and you yell at the dog. Your favorite place to stay is at Grandma's house because she makes you cookies and your room is always just perfect with flowers and your favorite games all readily available ..." and so on.

That is "Information Confirmation," and it is magical. C'mon—you know that! Don't you love it when somebody was actually listening to what you said? Doesn't it make you feel cared for, loved, and respected? Doesn't it make you appreciate and even trust that other person just a little bit more? Oh, what's that? This takes too much time and trouble? How effective have you been lately in getting people to want to do what you want them to do? Maybe you should take the time ...

Now your child is as relaxed as you want him or her to be. Now you want to begin relating the features of room cleaning and organization to their very words about losing stuff, Grandma's house, and taking on big tasks and breaking them into smaller, bite-size pieces and to offer up Trial Closes.

"How about if the first thing you do is to simply pick up your loose clothing off the floor first? Would that be so difficult?"

You have to get his buy-in to your idea one step at a time. He has to see how he has a need to do what you suggest. He needs to feel task tension within himself. That inner tension comes from his realization that you are correct. He needs to take an action to improve his problem.

It does not matter if you are selling private jets or just convincing your friends to go bowling instead of seeing a movie. *It's all the same!*

We cannot force people to do our will by coercion, fear tactics, threats, or pleas. They will only take an action if it is their best interest. They must respect you. They must sense that you genuinely care about them. They must be relaxed enough to listen. You *must* ask questions about them, questions that are pertinent to your end game.

Then you purposely begin rebuilding task tension by featuring your ideas and pointing out how your concepts will benefit *their* needs, dreams, desires, and goals.

"Hell, let's not go to a movie again, you guys! You just shared with me that the best times we have is when we do activities together! You just mentioned that you feel best when you're being active and not building up your butts' fat cells. If we go bowling, we're not all staring at a screen in silence eating popcorn at a million calories a mouthful. We're talking and moving, sharing drinks and stories, and laughing and interacting. Let's go bowling tonight. You know you'll love it!"

That's "Advocating/Feature/Benefit!" Now Close them!
Some final words on task tension: *Stay on task!* Don't drift off in some nonessential direction to relax your target and be

buddies. You will never get your way or make a living at selling. You have a goal in mind. Stick with it.

Finally, with e-mail, tweeting, Facebook, and other modern tools, communication occurs in small bytes and out of the order of your agenda or the task tension graph. That is life. Interruptions occur. That's reality. As a sales athlete, always know where you are in your path of persuasion with a particular individual. Whether it's your child or a customer, know where you left off in the task tension department and pick it up at that juncture.

KEY POINTS

- ➢ Eliminating any of the six sales fundamentals from your presentation will compromise your results.
- ➢ Be able to skip around the order of the sales fundamentals in fragmented communications without missing any of them.
- ➢ Know where you are in your process and what remains to be accomplished as per the sales fundamentals.
- ➢ Task tension is one of your greatest tools. It is like the volume control for sound. Know how and when to turn it up and down for the correct effect.
- ➢ No Tension = No Sales.
- ➢ Every presentation, to be successful, must contain all of the sales fundamentals.

CHAPTER 10

Sales Fundamental #1
Meet/Greet/Warm Up—Relating

- ➤ You have a very short amount of time to make a lasting impression.
- ➤ No matter what they ask, do not launch into selling when you first meet customers.
- ➤ Meet/Greet/Warm Up is a "sales-free zone."
- ➤ It is not so much what you do and say as what you are thinking about your customers when you communicate with them.
- ➤ Customers can sense who you are and what you think—if you are confident or afraid, if you like them or not, and so on.

Subtle Psycho Synergistic Relationship

You only have about thirty seconds to make a positive first impression if you are talking on the phone or face-to-face, or even via e-mail. The saying that you only have one chance to make a first impression really does apply.

Why is it important to take as much time as necessary in the beginning and then ongoing throughout your presentation to relate to your customer?

What do you know about first impressions? Think for a few moments about all the great, good, and bad first impressions people have made on you. Why are first impressions so critically important, and how long do they last? What is it that we hope to gain from making a great first impression with our customers? What happens if we fail? How long does it take to repair a bad first impression? What is it that we are supposed to do?

Simply start with good manners and introduce yourself. Offer your customers a beverage. Make him comfortable. Ask him where he came from. Ask him how he heard about you. If you are on the phone with him or sending him an e-mail, ask him how his day is progressing. Care about him.

If you must respond to a triple-distilled double-A-driver personality's request for the bottom-line price of your product immediately after first contact, give him the broadest of your product's price range. Offer up an overview power statement and then get back to the real sales business of relating.

How you look (one hopes professional) or how you speak (preferably sober) are only aspects of a good first impression. The most important aspect when you meet the customer and make your first impression and of every meeting thereafter, whether via e-mail, phone, or live, is the quality of your intent and the passion of your inner belief. *That* is what makes a great first impression.

Here is what you don't do: *Do not sell.* No matter what they ask for, *do not sell.* As mentioned earlier, you can address their questions vaguely to appease them, but get right back to plain old common-sense good manners. Offer a drink and a comfy seat and find out where they come from; ask them how their day is going. Then be conversational. Find common ground from which you can relate, be it restaurants, children, weather, activities, and so on.

That is all good stuff, but again, it is *not* what makes for a great first impression. What if I told you that while you have undoubtedly made hundreds, if not thousands, of great first impressions, you haven't hit on the complete reason why you made those great first impressions in your life?

Use your consciousness with purpose and discipline, just like Lord Olivier did when he excited that audience on *The Tonight Show* by doing virtually nothing except to *direct and focus the strong discipline of his trained consciousness.*

And what is it that you should be projecting through your focused concentration at this first stage of interaction (live, phone, or e-mail)? Find something you can love about this customer. It does not matter what that is: the way he laces his shoes, the sound of his voice, or the words he strings together in his e-mail responses. Find something you like about him and focus on that! If you *DO* that for your customers you will *HAVE* them attracted to you. Genuine caring and confidence attract. *BE* those things. All the while continue to "chit-chat" until you feel a comfortable relationship. That is the path to a great Meet/Greet/Warm Up. That is Selling Basic #1.

The same fundamental can be applied in your e-mails as well. What you say in an e-mail is an extension of your voice and your mind's emotional content when you write it. Craft your e-mails carefully. Make each word count! Write from your heart.

How do you think your customer assesses you on a first-impression basis? What are the criteria by which he will judge you?

Imagine how powerful you could be if you were consciously competent about what really makes a great first impression. What is the #1 most primary aspect of making a great first impression?

What we are BEing within is what your customers will "pick up on" far more than anything you DO or how you look. We call this reaction between people a "subtle psycho synergistic relationship."

The UPS Man, the FedEx Man, and the Dog

There was a dog named Cowboy—a very big dog, about eighty-five pounds of solid setter/Dalmatian/hound muscle wrapped up in a white package with pale beige spots all over. He wasn't a particularly good dog or a smart dog, nor was he a particularly bad dog or a stupid dog. For the purpose of this story, Cowboy was quite simply a dog's dog.

Cowboy lived out in the country in Montana at the end of a long gravel driveway leading to a house on a tiny lake nestled in pine-scented woods. From time to time the peace and serenity of that scene would be disturbed by a large delivery truck coming up the gravel toward the house. Sometimes it was the UPS man delivering packages. Sometimes it was the FedEx man doing the same. They both drove large trucks about the same size. They both wore uniforms. They both delivered packages. They both carried a good supply of dog treats to make friends with all the dogs along their routes.

In fact, the only palpable difference between them was the different colors of their truck and uniforms, but that shouldn't matter to a dog, because dogs, after all, are allegedly color blind.

Well, as life has its peculiar ways, Cowboy *loved* the Fed Ex man and *hated* the UPS man.

When the FedEx man came up the driveway, he would honk his horn a couple of times quickly to announce his arrival and go into the back of his truck to collect the parcel, and on the way out of the truck he would grab a dog treat (usually a little dog biscuit) and throw it to Cowboy, who waited patiently with his tail wagging and with a big "grin" on his face. Cowboy would eat the biscuit in one gulp and follow the FedEx man to the front door and back to his truck, all the while with his tail wagging.

When the UPS man came up the driveway, he would honk his horn a couple of times quickly to announce his arrival and go into the back of his truck to collect the parcel, and on the way out of the truck he would grab a dog treat (usually a little dog biscuit) and throw it to Cowboy. That is where the similarity ends. Cowboy was not patiently waiting with his tail wagging. Instead Cowboy was waiting to demonstrate just how terrifyingly vicious eighty-five pounds of solid dog muscle could be. He would refuse the biscuit, bare his large teeth, and with his fur up he would snarl, growl, and bark at the UPS man, who would call helplessly from his truck for someone to come from the house to collect the package from within the safety of his vehicle. This went on for years and years until Cowboy finally got too old and weak to care about such things anymore.

What was going on with the dog and the delivery men?

Doesn't it seem to have a lot to do with things other than how they looked, spoke, and behaved? What we are *BEing* within is what your customers will "pick up on" far more than anything you *DO* or how you look. We call this reaction between people a "subtle psycho synergistic relationship."

No customer walks into your store, e-mails you, or calls you on the phone to find out if he is impressed with you or if he even cares about you. The fact of the matter is that he would prefer if he could avoid talking to you altogether.

Eight out of ten customers are going to put up smoke screens and barriers so that they won't have to talk to you much at all. By the way, the other two out of ten customers are probably lonely "amiables" or "expressives" who just want someone to talk to, and they picked you.

Those eight out of ten customers put up their defenses by walking into your store or calling or e-mailing and asking two or three questions:

"Do you have a brochure you could give or send to me?"
"How much does it cost?"
"What will it do for me?"
"I'm just looking."

They say these things because they don't want to talk to you. If you skip Sales Basic #1 and respond to them by selling, you may as well thank them for their time and say good-bye. If selling were easy, we would just lay out a pile of brochures and contracts and do business via self-serve.

So much of our business is done via e-mail and/or phone. How does one go about making a great first impression on the phone or, even more difficult, via an e-mail contact? Can that even be done?

How do we account for the existence of great writers and mediocre writers? Why are some books so staggeringly effective on our emotions and others are not? What makes a great writer great? What makes a bad writer bad? They all use the same letters. They all use the same words. They all tell stories or give some form of information.

A great writer's "secret sauce" is locked into their written word. Their skill, passion, belief, and focus bore the words you see on their pages. The way they weaved their thoughts together into words and sentences resonates with their power of focus as they wrote. It is the same for sales athletes when you write your e-mails.

It bears repeating. To be great in an instant, to make a great first impression, and to convey greatness of power regardless of the situation requires the discipline to be able to manifest quality of intent, vulnerability, razor-like focus, and emotional availability to the task at hand.

KEY POINTS

- ➢ You have less than a minute to make a lifelong impression.
- ➢ Do not launch into selling no matter what the customer asks; focus on creating relationship and commonality.

- ➢ The customer can "sense" what is going on inside you. Sometimes what you are thinking when you communicate is more important than what you actually say or do.
- ➢ Are you confident and friendly inside or nervous and uncomfortable?

CHAPTER 11

Sales Fundamental #2
Intent Statements—Control the Contact

> ➤ Intent statements allow you to maintain control of the contact.
> ➤ Tell your customer what you are going to cover in the communication.
> ➤ Maximize the small amount of time you may get from your time-crunched customers by directing the focus of the communication and setting up a second contact.

Why an intent statement? What is it and why is it important? What do we, as sales athletes, hope to gain from a great intent statement?

We all know the old sales adage that states, "Tell them what you are going to tell them, then tell them, then tell them what you just told them."

Essentially, the customer is uncomfortable. Remember that it took some courage for her to enter the pack of wolves we salespeople have a reputation of being.

She does not know what to expect, so fear of the unknown is operating no matter how great her first impression of you may be. Once you feel you have made a great first impression, you need to relax your customer and make her comfortable by telling her what to expect.

Additionally, you are disarming a natural desire to control the agenda. We are all more comfortable when we feel in control. By delineating how things will proceed with an intent statement, you are taking control of the meeting agenda and easing your customer's fear of the unknown.

Remember that even if you made a great first impression, the customer will still be more comfortable if she could simply obtain bottom-line facts and a brochure and leave your shop.

Remember Cowboy the Dog and the UPS man? Your state of mind (what you are thinking) is what they will react to most when you are speaking. So first off, when you are about to embark on your intent statement, make certain it is coming from a position of genuine caring for the comfort of your customer. That is the *BEing* part. Be caring.

Now what do you need to do with your intent statement, or rather, what does your intent statement need to do for you?

There will need to be intent statements for the first contact as well as for all follow-up calls/e-mails right up to your final contact with a customer. Each time we reengage with a customer for a specific purpose, it will be a good idea to outline, after first relating again, the purpose of the contact. That creates a context within which the conversation can unfold.

In the old days, your customer would walk into your store and you would commence with a great sales presentation using some variation of the six sales fundamentals.

Wait! Did you hear that "whooshing" sound? That was the old days flying past. Adios, days gone by!

Now if we are lucky enough to speak to a customer in person, he already knows as much about our product as we do before he walked in the door. More often than not we are dealing with a customer via the eight-hundred-pound gorilla of preference—e-mail. Or, too often, we are talking to him on his mobile phone as he drives to work or texting as he walks to his next meeting or drops the kids at soccer.

"Call/e-mail/text me back in ten minutes. I'm driving into a car park, tunnel, walking into a meeting, got to take this call ..." Sound familiar?

Now more than ever, making that first great impression and thereafter offering up mini-intent statements at the beginning of each subsequent communication is critical to stay on point, maximize the small amount of time you actually get, and stay in control of where you are in the presentation of your product.

Today one intent statement is no longer enough. Before making each contact, determine what you need to cover and what the end result should be. Your mini-intent statements should set up those requirements for proper execution. Here are the basic attributes of great intent statements:

Key Attributes of an Intent Statement

1. Gently segues from Meet/Greet/Warm Up to business agenda
2. Encapsulates what will be happening during this particular contact (in person/e-mail/phone call)
3. Asks permission on some level to proceed with the agenda: either the very next step, the contact itself, or the format of the communication (i.e., would you like to go over that now or shall I e-mail it to you, give you a chance to review, and then call you back in an hour)
4. Take away—this aspect is most effective when still establishing trust with your customer on the front end of the presentation. "If what I send you next doesn't excite you, this program may not be for you." However, when you take it away, *always* remember to give it back. "Usually after our members saw this,

they knew membership was for them. Maybe you will too!"

5. Trial close*—There are a variety of these to use depending upon the particular contact. Is it a full presentation via a previous appointment? Is it an agreed-upon follow-up call? Is it early on in the contact process, or is it a later stage contact?

*Trial closes can range from the subtle—"Does that seem fair to you?"—to the harder edge—"Do you feel this is an appropriate time in your life to take the next step?"

> *By delineating how things will proceed with an intent statement, you are taking control of the meeting agenda and easing your customer's fear of the unknown.*

In addition to the most important aspect of a great intent statement, which is genuinely desiring to put your customer at ease about what the purpose of your meeting is, a great intent statement must be very brief and to the point. It must also be relevant to the specific type of contact as shown below:

1. An in-person contact via a previously made appointment for a full presentation
2. A third follow-up call to review a specific interest
3. A final contact where the client has now reviewed all your collateral materials and the call is about moving forward with a purchase

What this chapter hopes to establish more than anything else is the importance of taking a moment prior to each contact to think through the desired end result and then to create an intent statement appropriate to that desired goal.

> ➤ Ten minutes is adequate time to cover any segment of your strategic segmented presentation. If you get the luxury of speaking to a customer, keep it short and exciting and always end with your intent of the next step. For example, at the end of the conversation, one might use a positioning statement like "It sounds to me that this product may work well for you. I will send you a small brochure. Turn to page eight and read that page. If you like what you read, send me a quick e-mail. If you don't like what you read, then this product may not work for you."

> ➤ Start with the next step already in mind. A well-crafted sales presentation always sets up the next step. One of the best places to use this positioning statement is your short intent statement. For example, "I am glad you liked what you read on page eight of the brochure I sent you, but I have a couple of additional questions that we have found important to our existing members. I can send you an example of some vacations that you might want to consider, but I am curious about how far in advance you typically make your plans."

Be prepared if you feel resistance from your customer or if he is attempting to crunch your contact for time. You can lead in with: *I only have a few minutes but wanted to ask you a couple of quick questions regarding …*

KEY POINTS

> ➤ Stay in control with strategic intent statements.

- ➢ Prepare the listener for the topic of your communication.
- ➢ Intent statements are the most effective use of the incremental time available in the busy world of today's customers.

CHAPTER 12

Sales Fundamental #3
Discovery—Diagnosis
and Then Prognosis

- ➤ Discovery is the most important sales fundamental.
- ➤ Creating need through strategic questioning.
- ➤ Keep it conversational and not interrogative, and listen twice as much as you speak.
- ➤ Never sell in discovery mode; your customer will stop responding to your questions.
- ➤ Reduce tension by getting them talking about themselves.
- ➤ By asking questions, you become more interesting to the customer.
- ➤ Feed the information they give you back to them in their own words.

Why do a discovery? That's an easy one. Imagine taking time out of your work day to go see a doctor about some malady that is making you feel unwell. You set the appointment. You leave work and perhaps have to use up some of your accrued sick/ vacation time to facilitate your absence.

You get to the doctor's office, and it is very busy. The assisting nurse greets you and gives you seventeen pages of forms to fill out. Then you wait well past your appointed time to meet with the learned doctor. Finally, the nurse escorts you down the hallway into a small cubicle with a privacy door. There she asks you to undress into a gown so that you will be ready when the "busy" doctor sees you.

You sit in the small cubicle uncomfortably, partly because your gown is ridiculous and open in the back, partly because the room is freezing and unfriendly, partly because you are uneasy about what will happen next, and partly because you are upset about having to wait so long past your appointment time to see this person, whom you have decided in anger to no longer refer to as "doctor."

Finally the doctor walks into your cubicle and shuts the door. He says a perfunctory "Hello" and then proceeds to write something on to his clipboard. He tears the paper off the clip board, hands it to you, and says, "That ought to do it for you." Then he leaves the room.

Dumbfounded and perplexed, you glance down at the piece of paper containing writing you can barely discern. The writing outlines two bits of information:

1. A prescription you must fill at the drugstore
2. An expensive bill you must pay

Disgruntled, you put your clothes back on and go to the front desk to settle your account.

What is wrong with this story?

That's easy. The good or not-so-good doctor gave a prognosis without an examination. Considering that your job is to solve your customer's need with your product, would it not be extremely advisable to do a thorough examination (discovery) before launching into selling your product (prognosis)? At the very least, isn't it simply good manners to do so? It also works infinitely better.

When Is It a Good Time to Do a Discovery?

Remember the old gangster films with Bogart and Cagney? One of the thugs would be receiving an interrogation "good cop/bad cop" style. Usually there would be a bright lamp shining onto the suspect in an otherwise darkened room. The cops would be pacing around the perpetrator, hammering him with one question followed by another.

"Where were you on Tuesday night, Jimmy?" "Who was with you to confirm your alibi?" "Do you think we're going to fall for that lame excuse?" "Who was the dame you were with?" "Does she have your kind of moxie?" On and on they would go until the suspect finally broke down in tears and admitted his guilt.

That is *not* what a great discovery looks like!

At worst, a discovery would appear to a rank beginner to be a series of questions following the intent statement where you asked permission to ask some simple questions.

A good discovery would appear to be conversational to an outside observer. The salesperson would be doing most of the asking in a nonlinear sequence. After the customer answers a particular question, the salesperson might respond in kind with a statement of commonality.

> *To be interesting, be interested. This is not a fake or pretend thing. It is not feigning interest but rather actually BEing interested.*

Discovery Process

> *Salesperson:* Considering that you travel with your children, how many hotel rooms or what size places do you most enjoy renting?

> *Customer:* We find that in order for us to enjoy the trip, we prefer to have at least two hotel rooms or a two-bedroom condo.

> *Salesperson:* I get that. It allows some time for actually being able to converse in complete sentences!

This goes over a bit more smoothly, more naturally. The downfall here is to beware of selling! The tendency, because it is so tempting, is to sell (prognosis) before finishing discovery (diagnose). You think you have something so you jump into selling, as follows:

> *Salesperson:* Considering that you travel with your children, how many hotel rooms or what size places do you most enjoy renting?"

> *Customer:* We find that in order for us to enjoy the trip, we prefer to have at least two hotel rooms or a two-bedroom condo.

> *Salesperson:* I get it. With our luxurious two-bedroom residences you can have your two or even three bedrooms. It allows some time for actually being able to converse in complete sentences! This is exactly what you two need to own!

Don't do it. Don't go there, no matter how tempting. Let us repeat: *do not do it!* If you respond to your client's answers with sales info during the discovery process, your customers will smell it. They will become more guarded in their responses to your questions. Worse still, they will begin to mistrust you.

A great discovery will also appear to be casually conversational to the outside observer. A great discovery in today's world may be segmented across numerous meetings and/or phone conversations, each time leading to, uncovering, or extracting the specific needs of which your client may or may not be aware.

So let's get back to the original question on this sales basic. Why do a discovery? (Remember the doctor story.)

Reduce Tension

Just as with sales fundamentals 1 and 2, we are still in the mode of building trust and reducing tension for the customer. Remember, he is still resistant to and concerned about being sold.

So what really puts people at ease and offers up a lot of fun? What subject are most people extremely comfortable talking about? Why, themselves of course.

Think of a social situation you attended where perhaps you were paired up with or sitting next to someone who talked about his or herself the entire time. What was your reaction to this?

How would you categorize or label that type of person? Have you ever come across a salesperson who did most of the talking? How much do you love phone solicitors who interrupt your day and dive straight into their pitch? Isn't that just wonderfully interesting?

Now think about a social situation you have attended where perhaps you were paired up with or sitting next to someone who asked you lots of questions about who you are and listened to you with genuine interest and then continued on, asking you questions and being enraptured by you.

To be interesting, be interested. This is not a fake or pretend thing. It is not feigning interest but rather actually *BEing* interested.

We can always tell when someone is *BEing* disingenuous. Rather, you must genuinely *BE* interested to be interesting.

How to Sequence Questions: Leading with "Yes" or "No" Questions

Start with easy-to-answer questions, moving toward questions that require explanation. Every question must have a reason and purpose. Carefully craft, position, and layer with a purpose in mind. This is *not* a casual conversation. It is a strategic conversation.

First ask questions that can be answered with one word:

- "Did you have a good day at school?"
- "Were you on time for classes today?"
- "Did you get homework?"

Then move on to questions that require explanations:

- "What do you typically do at school on Wednesdays?"
- "What do you usually do in homeroom?"
- "How much free time do you typically have in the school day?"

Then finally go to questions more specifically directed to your end purpose via layering:

- "Why do you often say you have no homework?"
- "Why do you think your teacher gave you a D in math?"
- "What type of effort would it take to move that D to a better grade?"

Now perhaps some key value-driver questions:

- "How do you feel when you see these math grades?"
- "Do you think you could gain some benefits by improving your math grade?"
- "What might those benefits be to you?"

Fill Your Quiver

If need be, take notes during the discovery. Preferably, listen intently and remember. The best waiters remember what you ordered whether you are a table for two or a table for eight. They listen and remember. They get bigger tips than the waitresses at Denny's. They are professionals.

Your customer is going to tell you how to sell him. Do not start selling. Just listen and remember what he says. Listen intently. Ask more questions. As a result, he will find you interesting!

In review, a great discovery contains the following five elements:

1. Reduces tension by getting your customers talking about their favorite subject, themselves! "Enough about me. Let's talk about you. So tell me, what do you think of me so far?"
2. Leads your customer through strategically layered questions to exactly the conclusion you want them to come to—your product!
3. Begins leading your customer via simple no-and-yes responses
4. Provides you with the information you will need later to make your sale. Or, if you will, it allows your customer the opportunity to tell you how to sell him.
5. Takes you to the emotional reasons your customer will purchase your product through layered

questions: Why is that? How does that make you feel? What does that do for you? This will bring you to his key value drivers (KVD), not just a grocery list of surface needs and requirements. If that is all you end up getting from your discovery, then you are a beginner, and you need to reread this chapter.

KEY POINTS

- ➤ Great discovery is the most important sales fundamental and your greatest sales tool.
- ➤ You cannot prescribe a solution until you diagnose a problem.
- ➤ Don't interrogate. Be conversational. Allow the customer to do most of the talking.
- ➤ Do not get a response to your question and then launch into selling to his response. The customer will close up on you.
- ➤ By getting customers to talk, you are making them more comfortable. We love to talk about ourselves!
- ➤ You become more interesting to customers by virtue of asking questions and listening intently.
- ➤ Repeating back to customers what they tell you in their own words establishes greater trust.

CHAPTER 13

Discovery's Key Value Drivers—
Finding Their "Achilles' Heel"

➢ Humans make buying choices based on emotional needs.

➢ Through strategic questions you must either uncover or create a need of which the customer was previously unaware.

➢ Layer your questions to get to the emotional reasons (key value drivers).

➢ Close on their key value drivers (KVD).

This is the element of discovery that separates the wheat from the chaff. The beginner will ask a grocery list of questions and receive a grocery list of answers, worthless without the key value drivers (KVD).

They would like a blue car with a sunroof and two doors that has a payment of around $200 a month and gets good gas mileage. So what?

While that kind of information could make you a sale, you will never run with the top of the pack. To be a superstar, never be satisfied with grocery list information. You are looking for the mother lode, the code, the KVD. It is their emotional reason the customer will purchase your product. It is their emotional reason that will facilitate a sale.

Let's consider your shopping habits. Why and when do you buy clothing, big-screen TVs, vehicles, cleaning products, foods, and so on?

What are the key value drivers by which most humans are motivated to take action and make a purchase? There are seven of them: health, security, sex, relationships, status, family, and legacy. Are there others? Possibly, but in our opinion these are the key emotional drivers. Bear in mind that status is a broad emotional driver. It can encompass a wide variety of symbols from wealth to intellect to power.

Okay, so if you agree on the fact that people, including you, buy for emotional reasons, how do you get the customer to that level throughout your sales cycle, whether it is one day or fifteen months?

What separates beginner discovery questions from great discovery questions?

Layering, layering, layering. Oh, did we mention layering?

Salesperson: Considering that you travel with your children, how many hotel rooms or what size places do you most enjoy renting?

Customer: We find that in order for us to enjoy our trip, we prefer to have at least two hotel rooms or a two-bedroom condo.

Salesperson: Really? That seems like it would be expensive. Why would you do that?

Customer: Easy—the kids can go hang out in their rooms, and Kelly and I can actually have an adult conversation with whole uninterrupted sentences!

Salesperson (looking at Kelly): And Kelly, how does that make *you* feel?

Customer Kelly: It reminds me why we got into this situation in the first place! (She laughs nervously.)

Salesperson (wait before responding to see if there is anything more she would like to add; if nothing more): I get that.

You now know by layering your questions with "Why?" and "How does that make you feel?" or "What does that do for you?" that Kelly wants more space in the interest of relationship.

Through layered questions, you can find the key value driver whose need will drive your customer toward getting your product. It doesn't matter if you sell pens or private jets; people buy things for emotional reasons, many of which they may not be aware. A great salesperson will make them aware of their needs through questions.

> *There are seven key value drivers by which most humans are motivated to take action and make a purchase. They are health, security, sex, relationships, status, family, and legacy.*

Using KVD to Uncover or Create Need

The job of the sales professional is to incorporate the overall picture of your product and what it does by identifying and advocating those key value drivers that are specific and relevant to your customer's needs and desires. KVD's complement the common needs of the buyer that appeal to their health, security, sex, relationships, status, family, and legacy. Applying KVDs to the buyer appeals to their conscious and subconscious mind. KVDs are common themes that drive people to justify a decision or position. Isolating these KVDs within your client can cause the buyer to move toward pleasure (solution) and simultaneously to move away from pain or dislikes (problem/need).

Key value drivers are somewhat predictable with most customers, so a statement from thirty-five thousand feet about what your typical customers look like has the probability of being received well by the current prospect. The following is a guideline that can help you to introduce, discover, and advocate the key value drivers on a personalized basis.

- ➢ Introduce in the intent/customer positioning statement an overall statement of the key value drivers of your product.
- ➢ Develop customer positioning statements: assume, relate, and position key value drivers.
- ➢ Continually reinforce and refer back to intent/customer-positioning statements.
- ➢ Predict and assume certain key value drivers but allow for the discovery to reveal the primary drivers of your current prospect.
- ➢ Identify and remember the key value drivers of your customer.
- ➢ Isolate the key value drivers of your customer.
- ➢ Advocate and reinforce how your product is relevant to the key value drivers that are important to your customer.
- ➢ Close on those key value drivers.

Support the customer's key value drivers with relevant third-party stories and appropriate sales collateral.

Uncovering and/or Creating Need

A great discovery leads the customer through questioning (the Socratic Method) to where you want them, which is to buy your product.

Let's be blunt here. Just because you have a customer who is inquiring about your product certainly does not mean that he is predisposed to purchase what you have. How many times have you gone shopping without actually buying anything or even desiring to? There are a zillion reasons we "window shop" and "kick tires." Maybe we are bored. Maybe we need to feel important. Maybe it's just fun to look, but we have no real need. Maybe we just want to make conversation or learn something new.

As great sales athletes, it is our job to uncover and/or create needs of which the customer might not be fully aware. This is done through strategic questions. How many times has someone asked you a question to which you responded, "Hmm, I never thought of it that way before"?

Questions are a great device for guiding choices without have to tell someone what he should do. Telling someone to do something creates resistance to the objective, whereas asking questions opens up vast unexplored fields of data in the customers' consciousness, which then opens them up to their own internal suggestions.

Don't tell them about your wonderful vacation concept or ask them a yes/no question like "Do you enjoy fine dining?" Rather, present an open-ended question: "Out of curiosity, if money were no object, what would be your ideal dining experience?"

Allow your customer to fill in the blanks that would otherwise remain missing.

KEY POINTS

> ➢ Find the basic emotional reason (key value driver) why your customer will buy your product; how

will it make him feel? What will it do for his emotional needs?

➢ If you can't find a need in your customer, then create one through questioning.

➢ Start with simple questions that require simple answers. Work your way into open-ended questions about "why" and "how," ending with questions about their feelings.

➢ You will use the KVD in your closing process and for trial closes as well.

CHAPTER 14

Sales Fundamental #4
Information Confirmation—Telling
'Em What They Just Told You

Information Confirmation—
Telling 'Em What They Just Told You

- ➢ Trust is positively impacted if you listen intently to your customer in discovery and feed it back to him at some point in his own words.
- ➢ Reiterate the customer's emotional reasons for buying.

This particular sales basic is subtle but critical and is best used as a seamless transition into advocating your product. The reason why it is so important is because it allows your customer to realize what he just said and that you were really listening to him. He doesn't care about how much you know. He wants to know about how much you care.

This builds further trust in your relationship and also softens the next step where you are no longer lowering task tension but rather are building it back up. The next step, Step 5, is selling. When combined with Step 4 it makes selling smooth sailing by linking the product specifically to the needs he shared with you. Some sales athletes like to go over the major items they just learned by immediately repeating after discovery what is important to the customer. Others like to "pepper" it into their advocating process by saying something like "You mentioned earlier that you ..."

Either way works well. The important thing is to be certain that you repeat to him those items that he told you were important to him.

Be sure to use his words and verbiage. The customer will remember what he said far easier than what you told him. Besides, when you use his own words, you are once again verifying your genuine interest in what he said and creating more trust!

> *Remember, the customer doesn't care about how much you know. He wants to know about how much you care.*

KEY POINTS

➢ Remember what is important to your customer and repeat his statements back to him in his own words when appropriate.

➢ Remember his emotional KVD.

CHAPTER 15

Sales Fundamental #5 Advocating—Finally You Can Begin to Sell

> ➢ Now is the first time you begin selling your product.
> ➢ When you launch into selling, fill yourself and your customer with your contagious enthusiasm.
> ➢ Pump it up! Your emotional contagion is critical.
> ➢ Be armed with passionate belief in your product.

Now it is time to begin selling. Remember that your presentation may be drawn out over a series of meetings, phone calls, e-mails, or texts. It doesn't change the game. You can't sell into a void. The doctor cannot give a prognosis without having first done an extensive diagnosis. Your discovery may have been mini-discoveries drawn out over a series of contacts. Maybe in each contact you sold after each of your mini-discoveries. Whatever the case, you cannot sell before you discover their need.

Now we are selling/advocating our product based upon what the customer has shared with us in our discovery.

Underscore his KVD in rich detail when positioning the elements of your product.

Passion and Belief in Advocating

We have all seen the contagious effect of laughter. I'm not referring to polite chuckling at a mediocre joke told by your boss, father-in-law, or work associate. I'm talking about that uncontrollable gut laughter that, if it remains unchecked, quickly escalates into gasping for air or coughing due to the excessiveness and depth of the contagion.

Just recently the media personality, Anderson Cooper, lost control in front of the camera while telling a joke on his news show. At first he began to giggle. Then he began to laugh hysterically, so hard that he started to cry. Guess what? The same thing happened to me, my wife, and two children who were watching the news show. We were infected with his hysterics and could not control ourselves.

We have all seen this on television comedy shows or film bloopers when the actors in front of the cameras simply cannot control themselves. Or better still, remember a time with friends and/or family when sitting around the dining room table and somebody does or says something that sets everyone off on a "silly spree," laughing so hard that someone doubles over while someone else literally falls out of his chair.

These examples are the rawest form of emotional contagion. The flip side of this emotion would be the tears of joy shed by witnessing the beauty of a kind act, a birth, or a wedding, or the tears of grief shared at the loss of a friend or family member. Anyone witnessing is also affected.

These are raw and passionate emotions that require little to no cognitive rationalization or logical thought process. These joys of life are the moments that literally take our breath away.

The passion and belief that we use as sales athletes is, by nature, different and more complex than tears of grief or uncontrollable laughter, but it can be no less contagious than those raw emotions.

Remember that we are acting (taking an action) in front of our audience (the customer). For sales professionals, this may be our eight thousandth performance. For the customer it may be his first exposure to our presentation and the product.

Nothing is more disappointing in the world than a speaker who lacks passion and belief. When we watch little children in second grade going through the motions of their school play, saying their lines by rote as the teacher showed them, it is charming as all get-out. Those little ones so often don't even know what they are doing, let alone supporting their actions with passion and belief.

However, it is a sad thing when it is an adult coach, salesperson, commentator, teacher, actor, doctor, dentist, river guide, or whatever, and they are so bored and tired with their "pitch," they are literally "dialing it in" while thinking about what they would like to have for dinner that evening. Their lack of enthusiasm will inspire the very same thing in us, boredom and disenchantment.

So just exactly how do we "pump it up" and perform our ministrations time and time again, each time making it feel to ourselves as though it were the first time? The question is much easier than the answer.

And to make it all the worse, in today's market we do not have the luxury of a linear performance from point A to Z. Remember that today's sales presentations can be segmented over short to long periods of time using a variety of communication techniques. So now we have the double whammy of not only needing to be on top of where we are in each communication, what intent statement we will use for the context of the particular communication, and what discovery questions we need to cover this time, but we also have the problem of having to switch out of whatever mode we are caught in from arguments with the boss or associates, auditing by the IRS, or that darn heartache of psoriasis into instantaneous and contagious passion and belief!

Why do we need to do this? If the client doesn't sense your passion and belief, he will be bored and underwhelmed. Translated, this means no sale.

How do we do this after the umpteenth performance of our presentation? Here's the way.

> *The passion and belief we use as sales athletes is, by nature, different and more complex than tears of grief or uncontrollable laughter, but it can be no less contagious than those raw emotions.*

Sophie's Choice

A long, long time ago, shortly after the inventions of sound and color were applied to filmmaking, there was a rather brilliant if not maudlin movie released, titled *Sophie's Choice*.

Okay, maybe it wasn't that long ago. It starred Kevin Kline when he still looked like a young Errol Flynn and Meryl Streep when she was still as beautiful and talented as she is today. In fact, albeit being in a maudlin tear-jerker "chick flick," Ms. Streep won an Academy Award in the Best Actress of the Year category for her brilliant performance in this piece of cinema.

Basically, the story line goes this way:

Boy meets knock-out beautiful Polish immigrant girl and her volatile, schizophrenic boyfriend. Girl is damaged goods. Boy falls for girl. Boy discovers why the goods are damaged. Boy and Girl make love. Girl returns to her schizophrenic boyfriend. Girl and schizophrenic boyfriend kill themselves. The end.

One box of tissues will not do it for most ladies watching this film. And most men will actually stay awake and may get a little misty-eyed if forced to watch the entire film.

Where am I going with this? I'm cutting to the chase. I'm cutting to Sophie's choice. In fact, the scene where poor Sophie has to make her tragic "choice" is perhaps some of the very best film acting in the history of cinema and certainly the reason why Ms. Streep took home so many awards for this film, from a Golden Globe to Critic's Choice to an Academy Award.

The scene itself is gruesome, sadistic, and essentially horrible. I apologize for walking down this path, but there is a reason Ms. Streep nailed this scene. Much like Lord Olivier's earlier example from *The Tonight Show with Johnny Carson*, her ability to foster passion and belief in her work are unparalleled.

Sophie is on her way to a concentration camp with her two very young children, a charming son of about seven or eight and a beautiful little daughter of around five or six.

She is stopped by a nasty SS border patrol unit for a credentials check.

Being a very bad and sadistic man, the SS officer tells Sophie that she can pass through to the camp on one condition. Right then and there she must turn one of her two children over to the SS for certain death in the gas chambers. If she does not do as he says, he will shoot both of children in the head right there with his drawn pistol.

Sophie of course cannot choose. The officer points his pistol at one of the children's heads. Sophie pleads and cries hysterically. The officer relents and tells her to choose.

This long scene goes on and on excruciatingly. The children are hysterical, Sophie is hysterical, and the smug SS officer thinks it is all good fun for a day's work.

First Sophie offers up her boy as the SS officer drags him through the open car window with the terrified boy kicking and screaming. Then she changes her mind, pulling him back into the vehicle. The officer draws his pistol to kill them both. Sophie offers up her terrified little girl, and the officer pulls her through the car window, smiling sadistically.

Finally, thank God, the gruesome scene ends with Sophie driving off nearly catatonic with paralyzing emotions, the little girl screaming for her mommy not to leave her in the SS officer's cruel arms and the little boy sobbing hysterically from fear, stark terror, and the loss of his little sister. By the way, that very long and very painful scene was shot with little editing.

That was Sophie's horrific choice.

Now what the heck does that have to do with selling? Everything!

What does an actor do? Further, what does a great actor like Meryl Streep do better than most others? What did she do in that scene? Do you think that the children in that scene were also acting in the same caliber of Ms. Streep? Of course they weren't. They were reacting to what was happening in that vehicle and within Ms. Streep. In fact, it wouldn't surprise me if there were a therapist for the children just off-camera to debrief them right after the director yelled, "Cut!"

So again, why are we considering this? It is because of the depth of passion and belief on a very complex level that one person can conjure up in order to "spontaneously infect" all of those around her.

This is certainly not easy stuff. I can only imagine the level of rehearsal, in-depth self-examination and research, vulnerability, and emotional availability in the moment that went into being able to perform that one impossible scene when the director yelled, "Action!"

Bear in mind the amount of distractions on a film set. While we see only what is in front of the camera lens, there are dozens of people off-camera holding lights, sound equipment, cameras, makeup, monitors, and scripts. The focus of passion and belief for a great actor (one who takes action) must be laser-focused when the director tells the camera to start rolling.

Likewise, with our complex systems, products, and customers, when it comes time to advocate your product, the time for practice, study, and research is over. Whether it is via text, e-mail, phone, video Skype, or in person, regardless of what distractions are in your life at that moment, it is time to set distractions aside, create a laser-like focus of passion and belief, and *sell* your product as though it is the first and last time you will ever get the opportunity to do so! That contagion of power will shift right onto your audience (the customer) and get them excited! Be vulnerable and emotionally available for whatever level of enthusiasm bubbles up inside you. Let it out! Let it go!

> *When advocating, it is time to set distractions aside, create a laser-like focus of passion and belief, and sell your product as though it is the first and last time you will ever get the opportunity to do so! Infect your customers with your passion and belief.*

KEY POINTS

> ➢ Never sell until you are in the advocating portion of your presentation.
> ➢ When you do launch, do so with all the enthusiasm of a raw beginner, as though it were your first time!
> ➢ Pump up your emotional volume!
> ➢ Practice diligently, and prepare your ability to deliver with passion and belief. Be emotionally available to your impulses when presenting your product.

CHAPTER 16

So Just Exactly What Is Great Selling?

➢ Underscore the features of your product and how they will benefit your customers' specific emotional needs.
➢ Use baby negatives.
➢ Share relevant third-party stories.
➢ Incorporate power statements into advocating.
➢ Strategically pepper your presentation with trial closes.

Leave out everything not included in the list above. Amateurs, beginners, and dilettantes feel the need to tell the poor customer everything they know about the product; more often than not they confuse their customers or, worse still, create objections. If it is not part of the five bullets listed above, zip it and skip it.

Features and Benefits

It does not matter if it is pens or private jets, widgets or tripe-hunting traps. *Never* talk about the features of your product that aren't relevant to the clients' needs, which you uncovered in discovery. Why would you waste your time and theirs on such nonsensical communication? Keep selling brief and stay on point. Keep it "simple, stupid." Stay with and amplify the key value drivers. Eliminate the "noise" of insignificant sales babble!

If your customer wants a pen that feels silky smooth when he writes on construction paper and your pen has that capability, then talk about that and not how the cap screws onto the back of the pen so you don't lose it.

If he shared with you in discovery how it makes him look stupid in front of his partner every time he loses his pen cover (KVD - STATUS), then talk about the screw-on pen cover and leave out how silky smooth it feels when writing on construction paper. Get it?

Baby Negatives

Baby negatives are an excellent way to gain further trust with your customer. Never misrepresent what your product will do in hopes of gaining a sale. The truth always bubbles up to the surface. Misrepresentations will come back to haunt you. Under promise and over deliver on every aspect of your product. That is the way to gain referrals and customers for life.

Certainly you will tell them what your product does. You will also tell them what it does not do.

> *Customer:* Will I be able to exchange my resort credits for reciprocal use at other locations in the country?

> *Salesperson:* While you can do that, it is unlikely that you will ever be able to exchange for their high seasons. Those owners will have first selection of their high-season times.

Then follow your baby negative with a positive point in the same regard.

Salesperson: Having said that, you will have ample opportunities to go to the other resort locations during their shoulder and off seasons! In fact, if you have used up all your credits, you will be able to access additional use at our sister clubs for a greatly discounted rate!

Baby negatives are a must for creating credibility in you and your product and even further trust between you and your customer.

Third-Party Stories

Why have the greatest teachers of all time transferred their learning through storytelling? The reason is because it is much easier to learn from the indirect teachings contained within a story than to learn from a teacher who is simply telling you directly about life.

Stories are easier to process. They are less threatening to our personal belief systems. They take the lesson being given away from the speaker and put it into the format of a parable about someone or something else. As such, it is easier for us to digest them, draw parallels from them, and assimilate their lessons into our own experiences.

Did we learn best from listening to our parents and teachers telling us what to do, or did we learn best from observing things happening to those around us? Why is our culture addicted to the news? One of the reasons is that it is a great learning device. We can learn lessons and watch the consequences of actions unfold in the world around us through the experiences of others.

If your customer shared with you in discovery how it makes him look stupid in front of his partner every time he loses his pen cover, then take it up a notch. Don't just talk about the screw-on pen cover and leave out how silky smooth it feels when writing on construction paper. Tell a third-party story about how one of your customers got promoted when he took the initiative to replace all the pens with easy-to-lose covers in his office with your screw-on product and saved his company millions in lost pen covers! Be specific with the customer's name, the business he was in, when this happened, and what has occurred since then. A third-party story uses a parable to tie into the key value drivers of your customer (intelligence/status). Be ready and prepared to bring out a third-party story during every communication with your customers.

Power Statements

They say a picture is worth a thousand words. A good power statement about your product is worth at least a couple of hundred words.

What is a power statement? It is a different, concise, and more powerful way to state something.

> *Regular Statement:* If you work hard on your homework, you could get an "A."

> *Power Statement:* Imagine the respect from your teacher and friends if you pull an "A" out of this project. Universities will be chasing after you.

Power statements are not necessarily shorter statements. A power statement is a refinement of positioning. I would use the analogy of sap and syrup.

It takes nine gallons of maple sap, which is not unlike water with some sugar in it, to boil down to one gallon of the essential caramel-colored sweet thick syrup we love to pour onto our pancakes. Which would you rather have on a pancake or french toast—raw sap or syrup?

Power statements are the syrup of sales verbiage. They are essential statements with all the bland words refined out. Every sales athlete needs at least a dozen power statements that are ready to go, one for each aspect of his product, to provide a great sales presentation. By using power statements, a sales athlete is able to make stronger impressions on the mind, much like famous quotes, by saying things that customers will remember, as the following examples demonstrate.

> *Regular Statement:* While in residence, our members receive twice-daily housekeeping.

> *Power Statement:* The wives and mothers who are members here used to feel that their second home was just a second job.

> *Regular Statement:* We have a first-rate service department.

> *Power Statement:* If it isn't illegal, immoral, or unethical, we will provide you that service!

> *Regular Statement:* Considering what you receive from golf club membership, we are offering great value.

> *Power Statement:* Our club is not about the greatness of value. It is about the value of greatness!

Trial Closes

Trial closes are very similar to the thermometer a nurse carries around in her pocket. By using them, you can take your customer's temperature to learn where he is in his purchase tension.

Remember that once we begin advocating (selling), we are intentionally raising the customer's tension level. They trust us, believe us, and like us, but they won't buy if they are too relaxed. They won't buy if they are confused. They won't buy if they are bored, because we aren't being relevant to their emotional needs.

Trial closes tell us their temperature. Whether you are on the phone, e-mailing, or in person, use your trial closes to get a feel if the customer is with you.

"How would you see yourself using this camera, with auto or manual focus?"

"Would you be using the truck bed extender all the time?"

"Would you need the 125 or the 225 suspension for your rig?"

You are being assumptive by implicating their intent regarding some feature of your product. If the customer responds in the positive by relating to the question, you are on the right track, and he is interested.

If they respond with "Huh?" or "I don't know" or an objection, then you're going to need to figure out where you lost them or what their hidden concerns may be.

KEY POINTS

- ➢ Focus on the features of your product that relate to the personal benefits of your customer's emotional needs.
- ➢ Baby negatives create greater trust.
- ➢ Third-party stories are easier to assimilate than simply being told information.
- ➢ Power statements are worth many words; use them and talk less.
- ➢ Trial closes will tell you if they are still with you or if they have mentally "left the building."

CHAPTER 17

*Sales Fundamental #6
Closing—No Clothes/
No Eat/No Money*

Directing Action to Get Your Results

> In closing, no sales tricks are required.
> Use trial closes all through the advocating step.
> If you have done your job well, you can simply tell your customer what to do.
> A "no" just means you haven't gotten to a "yes" yet.
> There are only three real objections.
> Ignore false objections the first time you hear them.
> Never give up until the customer tells you it's over.
> You must change the deal before closing again.

Regarding closing, most everyone is familiar with the Pulitzer Prize- and Tony Award-winning play by David Mamet, *Glengarry Glen Ross*. In the movie version, Alec Baldwin is the hotshot executive who comes into the broken-down, demoralized real estate office out in the sticks to give the team hell. He writes down on the board, "A, B, C," and asks them what it means.

"A—Always, B—Be, C—Closing. ABC, gentlemen. Always Be Closing!"

There are a lot of books with a lot of tricks that involve a lot of subtle and not-so-subtle closing tactics. I have personally heard hundreds of them. Most of them reek of tired, overused sales tactics and desperation.

Why? Because with plays, books, and films like *Glengarry Glen Ross* floating around out there in the universe dealing with all the flim-flam practices of silver-tongued devils called salespeople, most discerning customers today can smell a cheap closing technique a mile away and will turn you off in one flat second.

Besides, if you have done a great job on the first five sales fundamentals, using trial closes all along the way, you shouldn't have to resort to cheap tricks to get the sale.

There is a much better way to do it. They trust you now. They like you now. You have told them what your product or service will do, and you have told them what it won't do. Can you guess what the most natural and genuinely authentic thing to do is right now?

What do you do to get things "going" in your daily lives with your friends and family who trust you to advise them, things as simple as which restaurant to go to or what movie to see? Don't you sometimes enthusiastically "just tell them what to do next"?

Direct your customers. Make your recommendation for the next step. Be assumptive. Whether it is the second meeting, the eleventh phone conversation, or the twenty-third e-mail, at some point in time it is the exact correct time to tell them what to do.

Think about it—you have discovered their need. You have positioned your product. You have addressed some or most of their concerns (some concerns you simply ignore; see objections). The only way you will know if they are buying is to either tell them to buy or ask them for the order. They will either go along with you or they will offer up their objections to moving forward.

If they go along with you, stop selling and move on to writing the order. The easiest way to do this, and it is really not a sales trick, is to simply begin filling out, for example, a bill of sale at the beginning of your closing cycle. At least you will have the pertinent details of their specific purchase in writing with next steps and process precisely spelled out. If they sign it, great! If not, you can let them take it home to reconsider or e-mail it to them later as a reason for an additional contact.

> In today's economy, customers are not easily swayed by urgency tactics. They know that your offer will still be available tomorrow.

Closing Key Attributes

1. Recommendation
2. The next step is ...
3. Handling objections
4. Changing the deal
5. Closing again

Handling Objections in Closing Mode

If your customer offers up objections to moving forward, you need to boil those objections down to several categories you can actually work with. "Thinking about it" is not something you can work with, so you must make it relevant. Even if he really does "need to think about it," you need to narrow that concept down to several categories with which you can work. Again, you cannot work with "think about it." Thinking about it means different things to different people. You need to discover what it means to your customer. In today's economy, customers are not easily swayed by urgency tactics. They know that your offer will still be there tomorrow.

Real Objections

1. **The Product:** They are not convinced about some aspects of your product or it does not fit their needs as discussed.
2. **The Money:** They are concerned that your product is not affordable and are embarrassed to tell you that, or that it is not of relevant value to them.
3. **The Timing:** Is now really the best time to move forward? When may it be a better time? What is in the way? Surgery, divorce, college, death?

While each of these three "real" objections can be broken down into smaller parts, these are the only objections that are real enough for you to work with.

How do you take a false objection and narrow it down to one of the three categories?

Usually, Mr. and Mrs. Smith, when someone tells me they need to think about it, they are talking about one of three things. Either they are not convinced about [the product], they do not feel the cost is relevant to the gain, or the timing is not quite right. Which of these three things resonates most with you?

Further, what objections (false objections) can be ignored or put off until later to see if they resurface and are indeed real concerns?

That is an excellent question/point, Mr. Smith. You know, I don't have the exact answer for that right now, but I will certainly get it for you later!

If the objection does not come up again later, it was probably not real or is of minor concern that is no longer relevant.

Essentially, whether during the same meeting in person, on the phone, or over an extended period of time, you keep chipping away at closing your customer. Never give up unless they tell you to. If your customer does not tell you to give up or leave them alone, then keep stepping up to the plate! Just follow the rules above.

Remember, you cannot ask for the sale again if you haven't changed the deal. That is "grinding" the issue. It is the surest way to irritate your customers and lose them forever. *Every time you are able to change the deal, you are then able to once again reinitiate a closing process.*

KEY POINTS

- ➤ Today's customers are quite familiar with "closing tactics."
- ➤ Trial closes through the advocating process should have pulled out most of your customer's concerns.
- ➤ If you have done your job well you should be able to simply tell them what to do next.
- ➤ Never take the first "no" as the last "no."
- ➤ There are only three real objections. Everything else is a false objection.
- ➤ Unless you hear a false objection more than once, ignore it.
- ➤ If the customer says they are done, then you are done.
- ➤ Sales athletes always work in a "no-grind zone!"

CHAPTER 18

Attitude—The Eight-Hundred-Pound Gorilla

➢ Thoughts are things. They manifest your reality.

➢ Negativity creates a negative world.

➢ Love and gratitude is the antidote to "stinkin' thinkin'."

➢ Positive attitude is not something that can be turned on and off at will. It is a chosen path of personal culture, a learned habit of behavior.

Thoughts are things! Your attitude will impact your lives at every level: health, friendships, domestic relationships, career—everything!

If we are negative with the "!*@!!?@ drivers" as we commute to work or the "darn husband/wife" we have to deal with or the "crazy people next door and that dang dog of theirs," how do we switch into a game mode of positive attitude at the front door of our career establishment? That is a risky game to play. Negativity is contagious, not only to those around us, but also to ourselves. It can set up a downward spiral from which only a truly life-changing event can motivate us to recover.

Think of the Dickens classic, *A Christmas Carol*. That was the author's treatise on negativity and how it made Ebenezer

Scrooge's world become so very small that the only way he could escape it was to witness his own death and the lack of caring from anyone who knew him. That is with the exception of his nephew, who insisted on toasting him Christmas Day after his death, and Tiny Tim, who insisted in blessing him at their meager Christmas table.

Those two small moments of "love" were all that was required to lift old Ebenezer out of his fate. He felt grateful for their loving thoughtfulness. And that is exactly the way to lift ourselves out of negativity into a constant pattern of positivity. Gratitude and love are the superhighways to attitude adjustment. However, those two states of being require strong discipline of thought:

> Be mindful of your thoughts.
> They become your words.
> Be mindful of your words.
> They become your actions.
> Be mindful of your actions.
> They become your destiny!

Negativity is contagious. It can set up a downward spiral from which only a truly life-changing event can motivate us to recover.

It is only possible to have a great attitude through disciplined practice and the constant nurturing of an attitude of gratitude. BE grateful.

The Pony

There was a historic gathering of all the world's most notable psychiatrists, psychologists, and psychotherapists for the purpose of understanding positivity in humans, its effects on the outcome of events in our lives, and how to discern it as a predictive behavior.

In one of the most famous experiments during this series of case studies, two boys aged twelve were selected. One boy, it was determined, had the very worst attitude of all the other subjects in his age group. He was cantankerous, ungrateful, negative, and full of blame for everything in his life.

The other boy was selected for the opposite attributes. He lived within a context of taking primary responsibility for experiences in his life. He was also grateful, gracious, full of laughter with a keen sense of humor, and generally fun to be with.

On different days, each boy was taken into the same room with a therapist who handed each a shovel without saying a word. When the boys would ask the purpose of the shovel, a portion of the wall was lifted into the ceiling, revealing a large plate glass window into another room. Again no words were spoken. After some time, each of the two boys would approach the window, the positive subject doing so in one-fifth less time, and look into the other room and ask, "What's that?"

The therapist would announce that it was a room waist-deep full of horse manure. She would then go on to explain that the purpose of the shovel was for the boy to go into that room and empty it of its contents. Each boy asked, "Why?"

The therapist explained that if the room were emptied of its contents, there might be a prize given of a very special toy. Then again, there might not be a prize.

When the subjects considered the task at hand, they both inquired what the prize would be, *if* there even was one. They were told that the only way to find that answer was to begin shoveling and complete the required task.

The following day, the negative subject went first, complaining all the way. It smelled. It was a mess. It got on his clothes. It got into his clothes. It was disgusting. It was a stupid task. There probably was no prize. It was just a dumb trick. If there was a prize, it certainly wasn't going to be worth this horrible mess.

The shovel was too small. The manure was too wet. The room was too hot. There wasn't enough ventilation, and on, and on, and on ... So much complaining occurred that it took him approximately ten times longer over a two-day period to accomplish the chore than the scientists had calculated it should take a healthy boy of twelve.

Once completed, the negative subject did receive a very special prize of a child's motorized scooter. When asked about the prize, the negative subject complained that he would have preferred another color, that one of the other kids in the experiment probably got a better prize, that the work he was forced to do wasn't worth the stupid gift, that the gift would've been better suited for a younger child, that the scooter sucked, and why couldn't he have a go-cart instead! And finally, he insisted that he did not want to be a part of any more experiments that were so stupid, messy, long, stinking hard, and boring.

Two days later, the positive boy was led into the same room full of manure. This boy exceeded all expectations regarding the unpleasant task ahead. Saying nothing at all, he began shoveling manure at an unprecedented rate of speed, all the while smiling, whistling, and singing to keep up his spirit and to keep his pace brisk.

The scientists observing the experiment were in awe of this individual. Before the boy could even finish the task, they called him into the other room. From their point of view, there was no need to continue. The boy was on track to finish the unpleasant job in about half the time they calculated it should take a healthy boy his age.

The positive young man stood grinning in front of the highly educated panel, covered from head to toe in horse crap. "Why did you stop me?" he inquired excitedly. "I would have been done in just a little while longer. Was I going too slowly?"

"To the contrary," the head psychologist responded, "you were brilliant! Why were you so excited and happy about doing such an unpleasant task? Why were you digging with so much joy and enthusiasm?"

"Are you serious? That's an easy one. You know why! With all that horse manure, there had to be a pony in there somewhere!"

Attitude—it's everything. It can turn a pile of manure into the promise of a pony!

Thoughts *are* things. To be successful, be disciplined with your thoughts and foster a strong positive attitude in your life. It is too difficult, if not impossible, to have a great attitude only when you deem necessary. It is only possible to have a great attitude through disciplined practice and constantly nurturing an attitude of gratitude and love.

KEY POINTS

> Your current reality is nothing more than the ending credits of what you have been thinking.

> You are the only one responsible for your reality. If you don't like it, change it by changing your thoughts!

> The way to change your life is by adapting a disciplined emotional position of gratitude.

> Positive attitude is not something we can turn on when relevant to our needs. It is a way of life!

> Negativity is the lazy person's way. It is easier to complain and be a victim than to take responsibility for what we experience. Positivity requires a disciplined choice of focus.

AFTERWORD

Selling in Today's Economy has covered everything for sales athletes from the six sales fundamentals to how those fundamentals relate to performance art. After all, that is what great salespeople do—they act via taking action and performing well!

This book took you through the changes you must embrace regarding the delivery of those sales fundamentals in today's time-crunched culture, where a sales presentation is no longer linear in structure. It is fractured, much like the production of a film, wherein you must always know where you are at in your presentation and relationship for when the customer says, "Action!"

You have learned how to create strategic, meaningful, and viable e-mails where less is definitively more, and you always end e-mails with a question to set up the next strategic contact.

Selling in Today's Economy has disclosed to you the power of love in relating to your customers and infusing them with your focused passion and quality of intent.

You have rediscovered the significance of mini-intent statements at the onset of each communication byte to frame the contact for maximum effect with the time you have been given, to maintain control of the sales process, albeit fractured, and to set up the next contact.

This book has reminded you of the gargantuan importance of a great discovery and how every time you drop one of the sales fundamentals from your disjointed presentations, the entire sales process ultimately suffers, rendering lesser results.

And finally, *Selling in Today's Economy* has discussed at length the critical importance of creating a discipline of positive attitude, not just when you are speaking with a customer but rather as your own personal culture in remaining positive. This enables the correct focus and passion of a meaningful life and the ability to manifest your desired results.

Sadly, as the saying goes, "We can lead the horse to the party, but we can't make it drink the Kool-Aid ..." or something like that.

And so it is true. Know less. Remain always the student. Have more wisdom. Nurture yourself through practice and self-discipline on the quality of your intent, on your vulnerability, on razor-like focus, and on emotional availability. Be the sales athlete. Revel in the rejuvenating attributes of constant training, learning, and growing, *always!*

Now get out there and start selling!